Vintage Lingerie

30 Patterns Based on Period Garments Plus Finishing Techniques

Jill Salen

Vintage Lingerie

30 Patterns Based on Period Garments Plus Finishing Techniques

Jill Salen

St Martin's Griffin
New York

Acknowledgements

Compiling these patterns would not have been possible without support from Philip Warren of Leicestershire County Council Museum Services (Symington Collection), Elen Phillips of St Fagans National History Museum, The Royal Welsh College of Music and Drama and Susan Hardy of Cosprop. Many thanks also to Christine Stevens, Margret Cross, Margret Pyke, Charlotte Hodgson, my editor Kristy Richardson and photographer Michael Wicks.

Many others have helped sustain and encourage me; Cissian Rees, Elizabeth Friendship, Don Moffat, Norman Leiter, Diana Humphreys, Sheryl Brittain, Joanna Burkill and Rebecca Salen.

More information can be found at www.jillsalen.com

VINTAGE LINGERIE. Copyright © 2011 by Batsford. Text copyright © 2011 by Jill Salen. All rights reserved. Printed in China. For information, address St. Martin's Press, 175 Fifth Avenue, New York, N.Y. 10010.

www.stmartins.com

Library of Congress Cataloging-in-Publication Data Available Upon Request

ISBN 978-0-312-64539-7

First U.S. Edition: February 2012

10 9 8 7 6 5 4 3 2 1

Contents

Introduction

Adorned in undergarments, the body is clothed, but not dressed; the body can be shaped by underwear, and the variety of intimate apparel available heightens its power.

For this book I had originally intended to research and collate information for brassieres exclusively, as I had done for my previous book *Corsets* (see Further Reading, page 124). However, I found this to be an impossible task since I had to include the other undergarments that were worn as well as brassieres, such as petticoats and garter belts. This book is a collation of vintage lingerie I have found useful and interesting as a costume maker, and most of the items recreated here are from my collection.

Collecting corsets is a very expensive hobby, but I have been able to collect vintage lingerie, or what could be described as "other people's cast-off underwear," from many sources including vintage fairs and upmarket garage sales, and gifts from people who know of my interest.

My collection includes items that are useful as a reference for costume making, or because they are so pretty, or the work in creating them has been so beautifully executed.

The term "lingerie"

Lingerie is a term for fashionably and possibly alluring items of intimate apparel or sleepwear. It used to mean "linen" in general, since originally all undergarments would have been made "of linen" before the importation of cotton in the 16th century.

The term lingerie is not used much until about the 1850s when it was appropriated from the French and was usually a euphemism for risqué underwear.

Why do we wear underwear?

The basic reason for wearing underwear is that society demands it. It surely would be the case that not to be wearing underclothes in the 21st century would identify you as poor or "naughty." As I walk down the street I am often treated to the sight of the waistbands of boys' underpants sporting designer names, occasionally girls' thongs and often bra straps, and often the bra visible through a girl's garment. Department stores have provocative underwear displays and we are bombarded in

Right: This deep, strapless brassiere from the 1940s is made by Symingtons (see pages 70–73 for pattern).

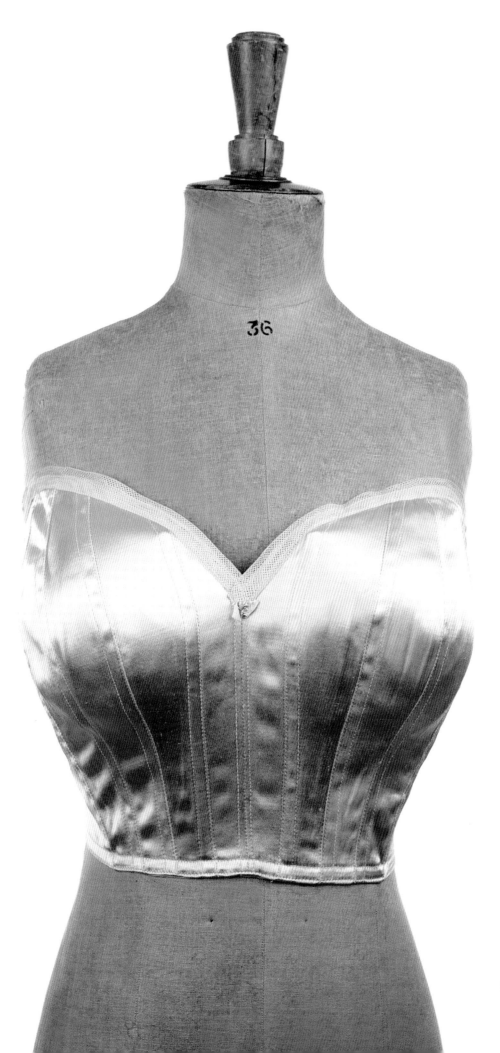

magazines and on screen with underwear advertisements. Who can forget the 1991 "Hello Boys" advertisement for the Wonderbra—a bra that actually started its life back in the 1960s?

One good reason for wearing underwear is to keep the outer garments clean by wearing an under-layer, such as knickers, that can be washed more regularly than the outer garment.

Another is to make the wearing of outer garments more comfortable, such as a slip acting as a lining, allowing the over-garment to flow.

Underwear also acts as foundation wear, such as a brassiere, helping us achieve a shape that we feel is desirable or that fashion dictates. Over the last hundred years women's breasts have been squashed flat, falsely enhanced, exposed, pointy, supported, and unsupported.

Lingerie in history

The wedding trousseau has now gone out of fashion but its original purpose was to start the bride on her new life, with clothes to wear on the honeymoon and during her early married life, and of course the size and cost of the wardrobe depended on the incomes of those involved. At the end of the 19th century there was a change in attitude and women's underwear became tantalizing—as demonstrated by details of wedding trousseaus, including fancy underwear, that were published in ladies' periodicals. From the 1850s we start to see underwear displayed in store windows and in newspapers and, with the advent of photography, women and men of the time began to be bombarded with visual imagery of lingerie.

In the past corsets were worn by women partly through choice but also under pressure from society: a corset-wearing woman was considered to be an upright, respectable member of society. By the 1870s there were those who felt that women in corsets and women not having the vote were linked issues—they felt that oppressive clothing that subjected the female body to inconvenient, unsightly, even tormenting control, also brought about the subjection of the mind. The rigorous attention to dress codes, the number of times a lady might have to change her dress in a day, and styles such as the crinoline or the bustle made almost any activity impossible. All this distracted women from the important franchises they should have had in many areas, including equality with men, the freedom to vote, the freedom to work and earn money, the freedom to be educated, and the opportunity to exercise birth control. The aesthetic feminists of the 1880s led the way by setting up organizations such as the Rational Dress Movement, which questioned the need for restrictive garments.

Women in the US were given the right to vote in 1920, and women in Britain shortly afterwards, in 1928. This coincided with a time when women had finally achieved freedom from restrictive garments and they were unhampered by their undergarments. They began to have roles in the workplace, they could take part in sports as men could and, possibly because women began to have access to birth control, they could allow themselves to be sexually alluring, enjoying attracting male attention and revelling in it.

Between 1900 and 1950 we see the biggest changes in what was worn as underwear, depending on age and occupation, with some items reflecting or supporting the outer garment. At various times in the 20th century fashion has also dictated the wearing of foundation wear; there was a resurgence of corsetry after World War II with the "New Look" and more recently there has been an interest in corsetry as outerwear, popular since the 1990s with its nostalgic look back to beautiful silhouettes and fashions of the past. In 1952 the film *The Merry Widow*, starring the glamorous Lana Turner, effectively sold corsetry to women once again; particularly black lace corsetry, such as the corselet or basque, which is called "a merry widow" in corsetry circles. The silver screen brought a vision of glamour to everyone and this had a huge effect on fashion with ladies wanting to wear garments similar to those worn by their idols.

Lingerie today

Beautiful lingerie can be bought today from most department stores as well as from specialists such as Rigby and Peller and Agent Provocateur, who are happy to take their inspiration from the past. Cosprop, John Bright's costume couture house in London, design and make costumes and have a collection of original garments, which is a resource base for what they produce. Also, Leicestershire Museum Services' comprehensive Symington Collection covers the years 1860–1960 and is a marvellous resource.

Practical note

This book is designed for the costume maker, who I hope will find the variety of patterns useful. When accessing the patterns, remember that no seam allowances are included; your experience should tell you what you need to add, but it is always a good idea to create a muslin to test out the pattern in an inexpensive, similar-weight material, before cutting into your precious fabric. Most of the patterns are 1:1in. The patterns on pages 13, 24–25, 32, 48–49, 80–81 and 112–113 are 2:1in. All of the patterns are shown half-size, so you will need to enlarge on a photocopier to achieve a full-size version. Grain lines, unless otherwise marked, are as the graph paper. Everything is as it was—in inches, but with metric in brackets for your information.

Pantaloons, 1850

Until about 1800, drawers were not usually worn by women. Men did wear "linings"—drawers made of linen, knitted wool, and even leather—for protection, warmth, and reasons of hygiene.

After about 1800 the fashion for a classic style of dress made of lightweight fabrics such as cheesecloth (or cotton voile), and often worn unimpeded by stays or waist slips, crossed the channel from France. It was widely reported that wearers would dampen their dresses so they would cling to the body; consequently having dispensed with their stays and waist slips the wearers required some modesty and took to drawers. These would have been made at home.

Initially—because it was accepted that men wore drawers and women wore nothing—when women started wearing them, it was thought highly improper, and they were thought to be immodest. Personalizing the drawers, decorating them into a garment no man would have ever worn, possibly made them more acceptable.

I have a variety of styles of drawers in my collection; the inside leg seams can be as short as 5½in (14cm) or as long as 11in (27cm). Some are finished beautifully at the lower edge, gathered and edged with exquisite whitework, crochet broderie Anglais or lace, perhaps with some expectation of being seen or possibly for the wearer's own pleasure. Cunnington call drawers, which extend below the knee, and pantaloons, which extend to the mid-calf, were often highly decorated and intended to be seen.

By 1860 it was expected that all women would wear drawers, trimmed with frills and needlework, and made from colorful flannel, a necessary garment by this time, as the crinoline was universally worn by society ladies and servants alike.

The pair of drawers from which I have taken this pattern has a waist that measures 30in (76cm) but can be pulled up to fit 25in (62cm) by a simple but effective two-tape system. The drawers are in perfect condition and completely hand stitched. They have been much laundered and could well have been made for the wearer's lifetime. They have a split gusset as is the case with many of the examples from this period.

By 1920 drawers were being referred to as French knickers if they had loose legs and directoire knickers if they were closed in. By the 1920s the term panties was being used and camiknickers (joined camisole and knickers) and camibockers (joined camisole and directoire knickers) were introduced.

Left: These embroidered pantaloons are dated from around 1850.

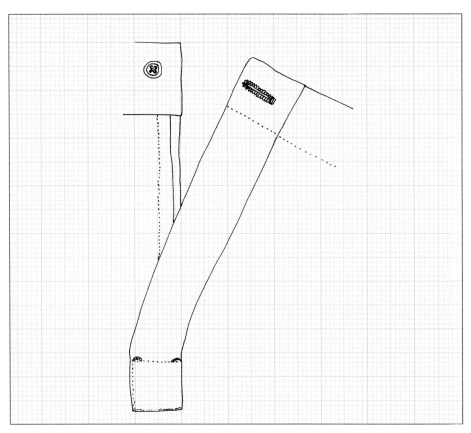

Detail of side fastening

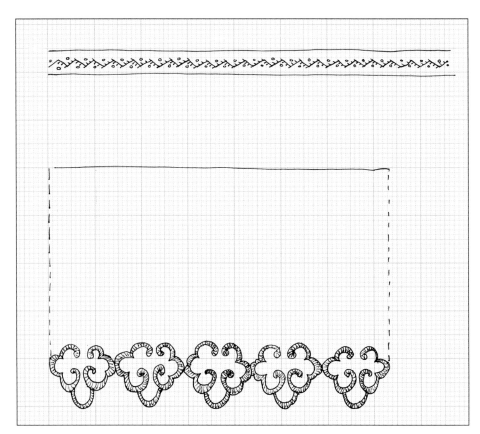

Detail of frilled edge in buttonhole stitch

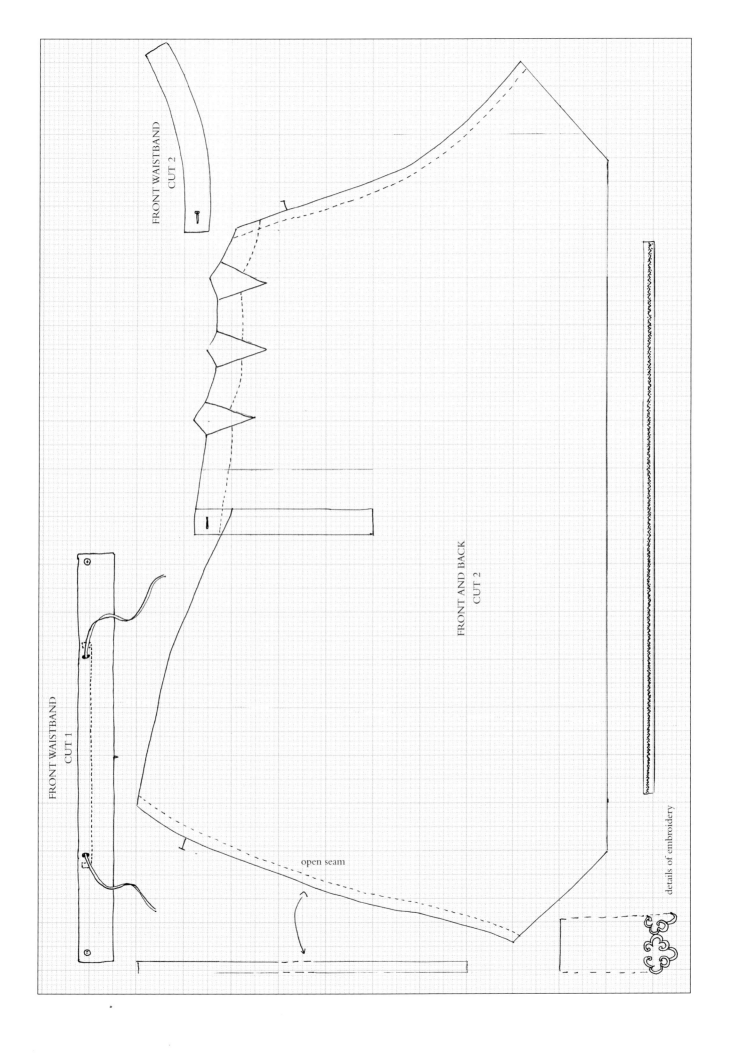

FRONT WAISTBAND
CUT 2

FRONT WAISTBAND
CUT 1

FRONT AND BACK
CUT 2

open seam

details of embroidery

Khiva Corset, 1890

This corset is in the Symington Collection held by Leicestershire County Council in England. It is an unusual corset; in fact one could almost consider it to be a brassiere as there is no suppression below the bust and the staining inside this item would suggest that it is a bust bodice to be worn during lactation. In Philip Warren's book *Foundations of Fashion* (see Further Reading, page 124), he describes this bodice style as being designed to fit on top of a specially made waist and hip girdle—presumably the strong snap fastener rivets with buttonholes above were to aid the fastening. Cecil and Phillis Cunnington, in *The History of Underclothes* (see Further Reading, page 124), describe waist slips buttoning directly onto the corset in 1878, so the practice was known.

But this garment, with adjustable straps and simple but strong closure at the center front allowing easy access for a baby to feed, is one of many nursing brassieres that Symington produced over its history. It does not look like a nursing brassiere as it is beautifully constructed and the buckles are as decorative as they are functional.

In 1875 the novelist Captain Frederick Burnaby, a famous swordsman and notable linguist, set off to cross Russia on horseback during the middle of the winter, aiming to reach the forbidden central Asian medieval walled city of Khiva of which it was claimed that "No man can storm the bastions of these walls". This could be the joke behind the naming of this corset.

This garment was created at a time when waist suppression was still extreme—almost the last gasp of the corset. It was a time when the Rational Dress Movement was beginning to be listened to with more credulity as women were taking part in sporting life, playing golf, bicycling, walking, and starting to find roles in the workplace, and this garment has some functionality. Respectable women would not want to go out uncorseted, but if still feeding a baby they would want to be able to do so easily and this corset would allow it.

Black might seem to us to be an unusual choice of color for such a garment, but it was not an unusual color for corsets at the time.

Above: Adjustable straps at the sides are as decorative as they are functional.

Left: The front of this Khiva corset shows the closure at the center front that would make breast feeding easier for women in 1890.

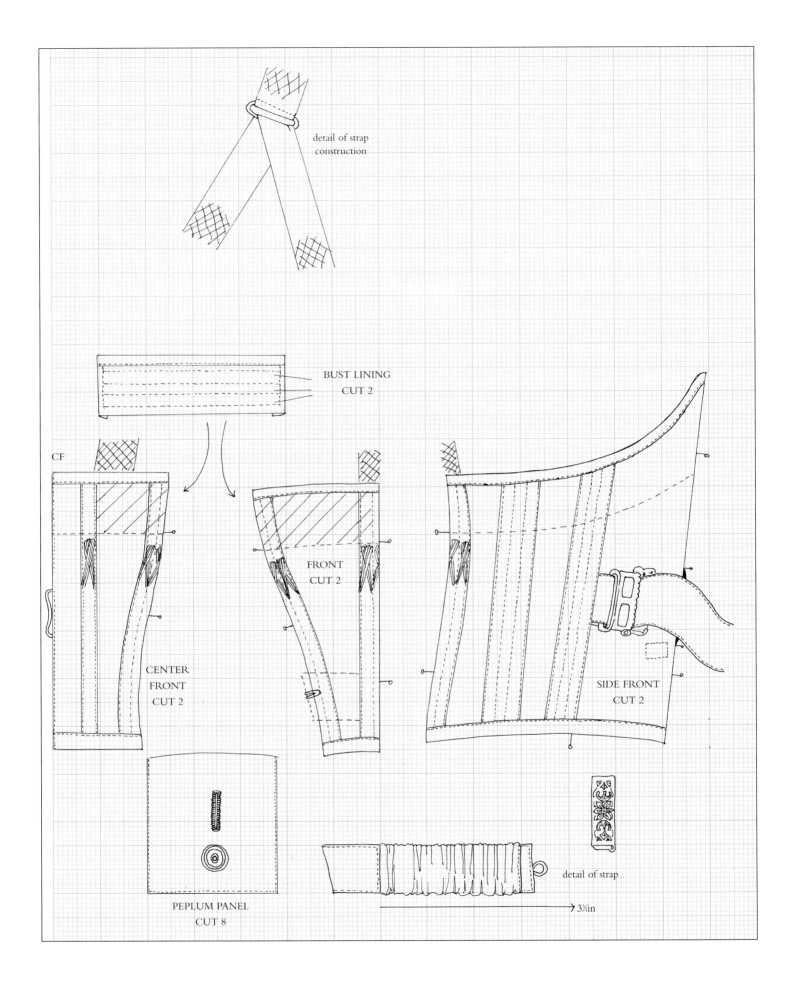

detail of strap
construction

BUST LINING
CUT 2

CF

FRONT
CUT 2

CENTER
FRONT
CUT 2

SIDE FRONT
CUT 2

PEPLUM PANEL
CUT 8

detail of strap

3¼in

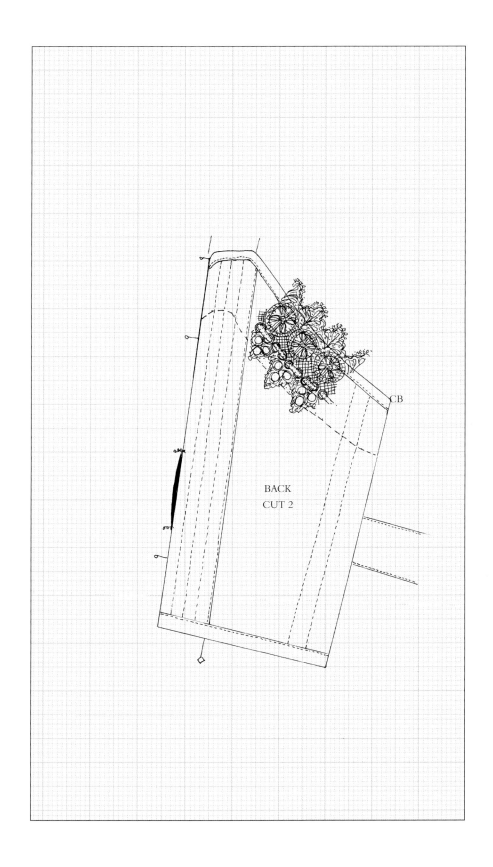

CB

BACK
CUT 2

Corset Cover, 1897–1905

From about 1880 the old practice of a chemise worn under a corset had changed: any or all of vests, bust bodices, bust improvers, and camisoles were now being worn. With the advent of women playing sports, finding jobs, and the beginnings of the active suffragette movement, there was less conformity and more underwear appropriate to the wearer's occupation or lifestyle.

Once underwear was on display in store windows and advertisements in magazines and periodicals, the practical, useful garment that had enough decoration to please the wearer became a very attractive, exotic garment, and by 1890 we are seeing "trousseau garments" emphasizing women's role in the bedroom as well as the lady of the house.

At the turn of the 20th century underwear in general was very pretty and often embellished by hand, with an expectation of being seen, as well as providing the correct base for the fashions of the day, as is the case with this corset cover.

The fabric is beautifully hand stitched, and embellished with eyelet embroidery, whitework, threaded silk ribbon, and shell edging.

Left: This hand-stitched corset cover, c. 1897–1905, is constructed in cotton with beautiful embroidered detail.

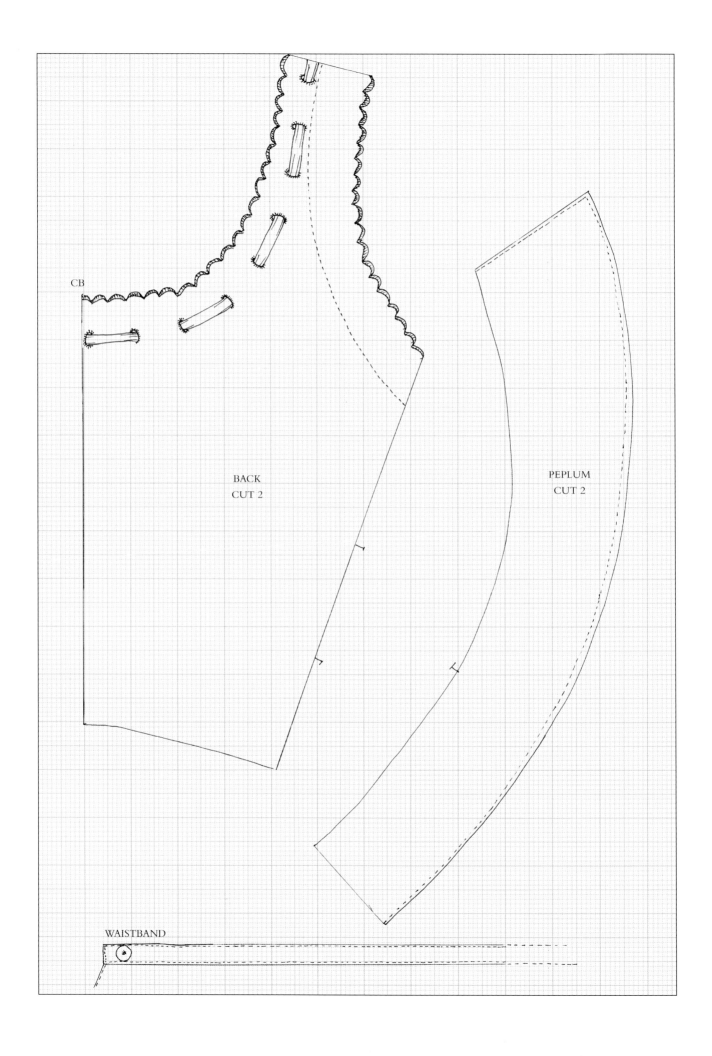

CB

BACK
CUT 2

PEPLUM
CUT 2

WAISTBAND

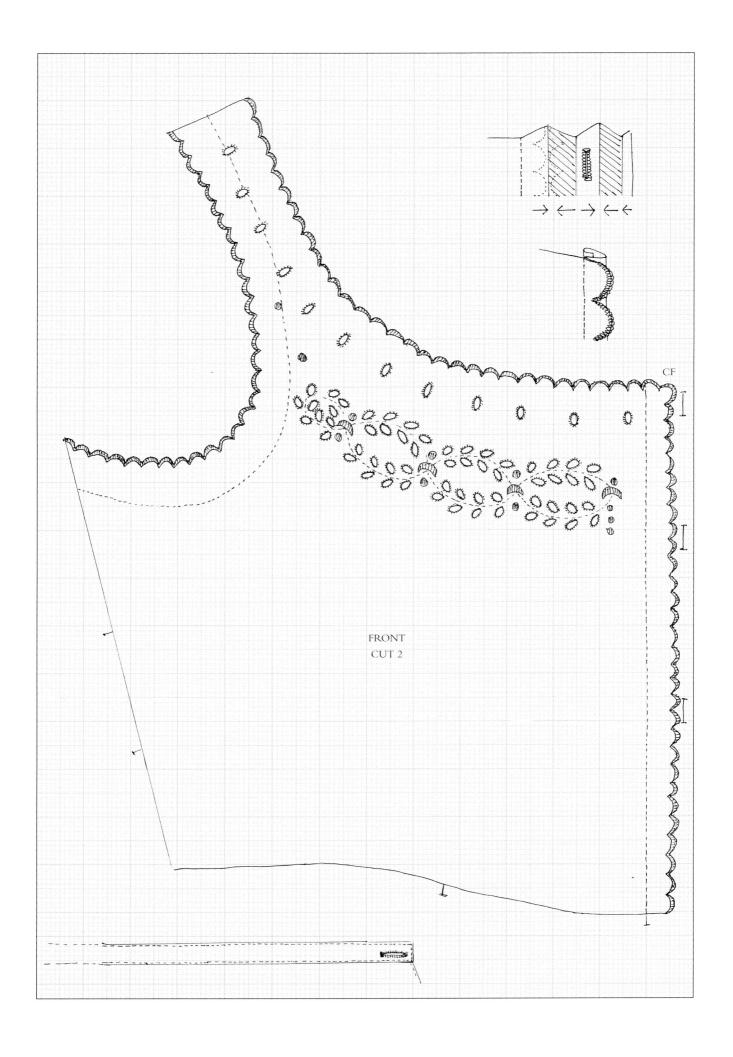

CF

FRONT
CUT 2

Combinations, 1900

In the book *The Workwoman's Guide* (see Further Reading, page 124), first published in 1838, a pattern for combinations is described as "Some persons, both ladies and children wear bodices attached to their drawers." There are some very interesting patterns for "combinations."

In 1870 the wearing of combinations became more common and they were available in cotton, linen, and wool, but could also be purchased in silk and chamois leather, to be worn under the corset. In the 1880s men started wearing Dr Jaeger's "union suits" (wool combinations), which were thought to be healthier.

Between about 1900 and 1910 combinations allowed a slimmer silhouette through the wearing of less underwear, and in England combinations, especially in silk or fine fabrics, were called camiknickers.

In the 19th century drawers and combinations mainly had open crotches. The closed crotch was thought to be improper, unhealthy, or perhaps to do with cross-dressing and, while they may be shocking to us, open-crotch knickers or drawers were thought to be modest during this period.

These combinations use a lot of fabric. They are made from the finest lawn and are almost transparent. The inclusion of delicate horseshoes in the embroidery indicate that they could have been part of a trousseau.

Left: Combinations from 1900, showing the open-crotch style typical of the garment during this period.

Right: Delicate embroidered flowers and horseshoes add interest to the edges of the garment.

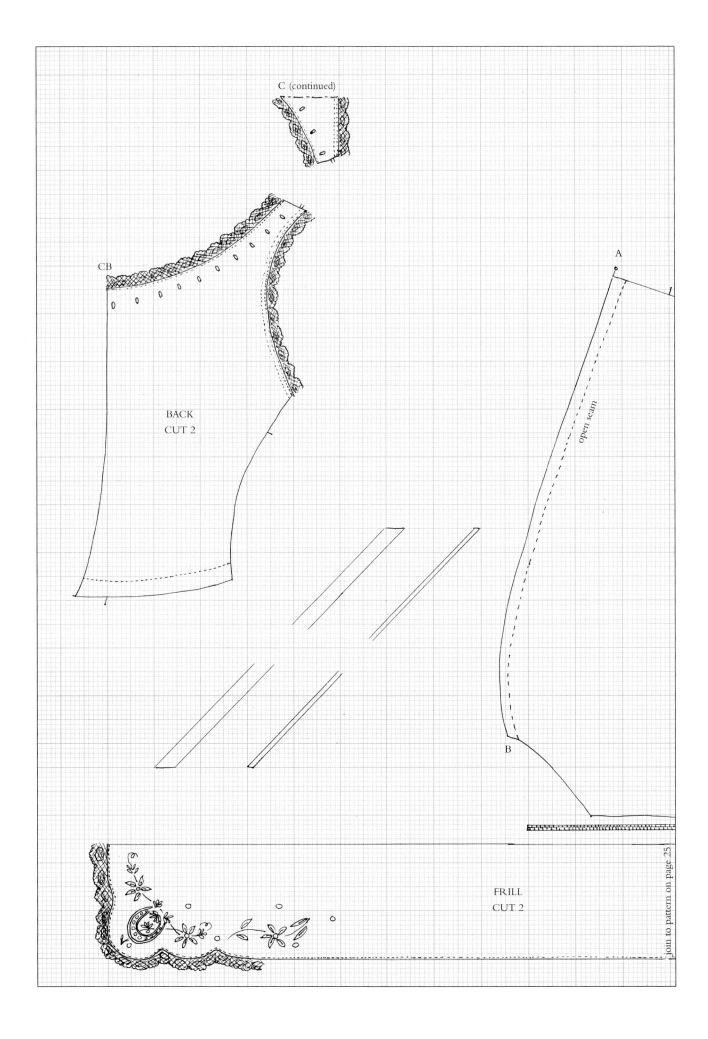

C (continued)

CB

BACK
CUT 2

A

open seam

B

FRILL
CUT 2

join to pattern on page 25

C

CF

FRONT AND
DRAWERS
CUT 2

Join to pattern on page 24

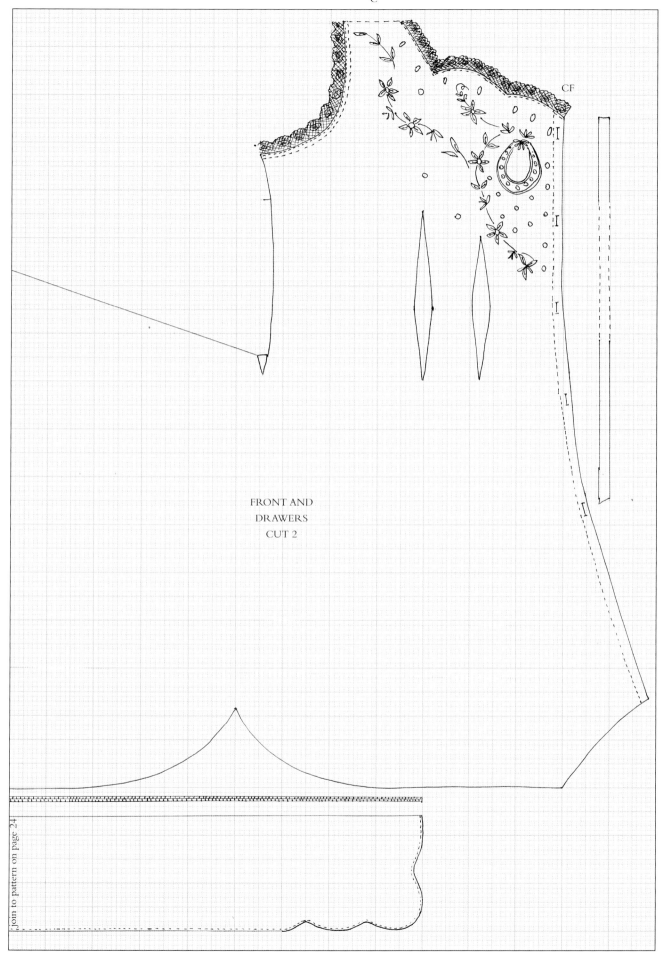

Tango Knickers, 1920s

These knickers are a very pretty example from John Bright's Cosprop, the couture house for costume, based in London. They are made in a loose-weave cotton or linen mix with an attractive lace inserted and edging the garment; they are completely machine stitched. The wearer would have had to step into this garment and, once in, would have to wiggle her way out again. One wondered how she managed to visit the ladies' bathroom.

After 1909 the fashionable silhouette of the Edwardian grande dame had slimmed down and by 1920 it was boyish or androgynous in appearance. Women had taken men's roles in the workplace during World War I, while the men were away fighting, and after the war not as many women would be able to marry as their mothers and grandmothers had before them because of the huge numbers of men killed. So we see the rise of the independent career woman who cut her hair short and went to nightclubs, without trailing gowns and pounds of undergarments.

Possibly the freedom women were experiencing saw some expression in their clothing; indeed the underwear of the 1920s can be seen as the start of underwear as we know it today, designed for comfort and practicality, attractive but also with a wide variety of style choices. For example, warm directoire drawers for the winter and flimsy silk chiffon for the summer or evening, not ruining or dictating the line of the dress, and looking pretty and even sensuous. Of course, what one wore would be dictated by many factors, including age, income, status, and occupation.

By 1914 there are references to tango knickers in department store advertisements; these would have a closed gusset and leg holes that extended up the sides allowing maximum movement when dancing.

By 1925 women could choose from a vast array of ready-to-wear underwear either in store or by mail order. B. Altman & Co. in America were offering step-in chemises, which were a similar shape to tango knickers, pretty and lace trimmed, and they also offered "athletic combinations," with closed or open crotch, knitted and untrimmed. Interestingly they also offered what is described as a dance set with a bandeau bra and "abbreviated panties."

It appears that the term tango knickers came from the craze for the dance of the same name, but the garments carried on, becoming known later as "step-ins."

Left: These 1920s tango knickers are held in a collection at Cosprop, London.

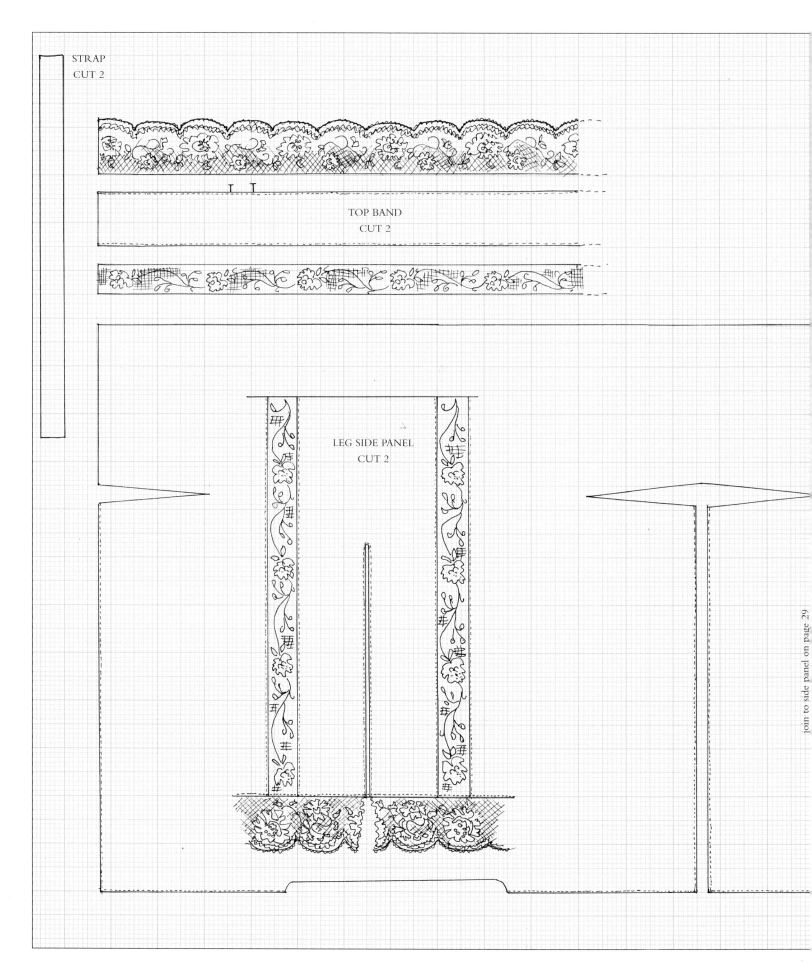

STRAP
CUT 2

TOP BAND
CUT 2

LEG SIDE PANEL
CUT 2

join to side panel on page 29

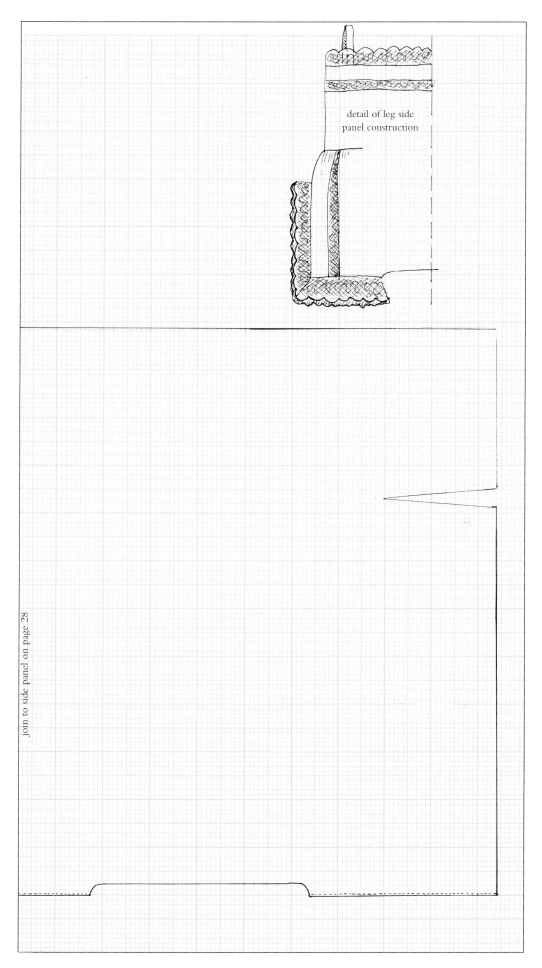

detail of leg side
panel construction

join to side panel on page 28

Lace and Chiffon
Brassiere and Knickers, 1920s

When I acquired this brassiere and a pair of knickers, I was told that they had been made by nuns in Ceylon. This would have sounded unlikely except that I knew the St Fagans National History Museum in Cardiff, Wales, has in its collection similar embroidered and hand-made silk brassieres, which were made by nuns in Ceylon 1920–30 and donated by Margaret Pike, the daughter of a couple who lived in Ceylon. Further research has uncovered that there were Belgian, French, and Buddhist nuns in Ceylon at that time.

The amount of handwork and embellishment on these flimsy garments is amazing; a potential maker may well be happy to use the pattern shapes but some of the embroidery and embellishment would be extremely difficult and time-consuming to recreate.

Left and below: These garments are constructed from chiffon, silk, and cotton tulle or netting, embellished by hand to stunning effect.

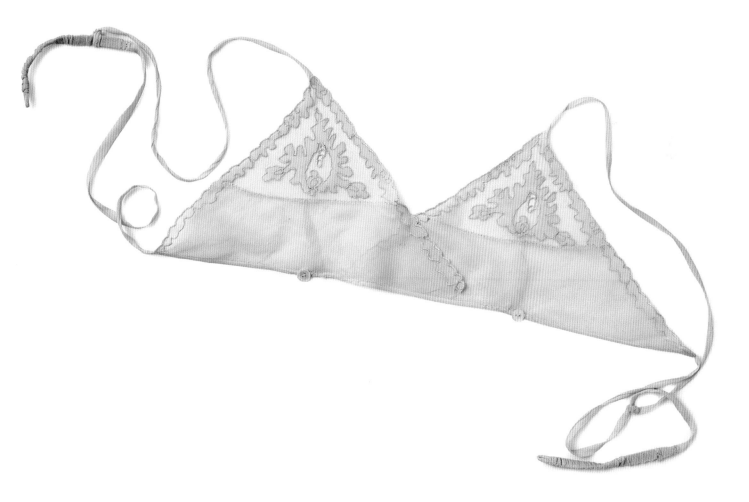

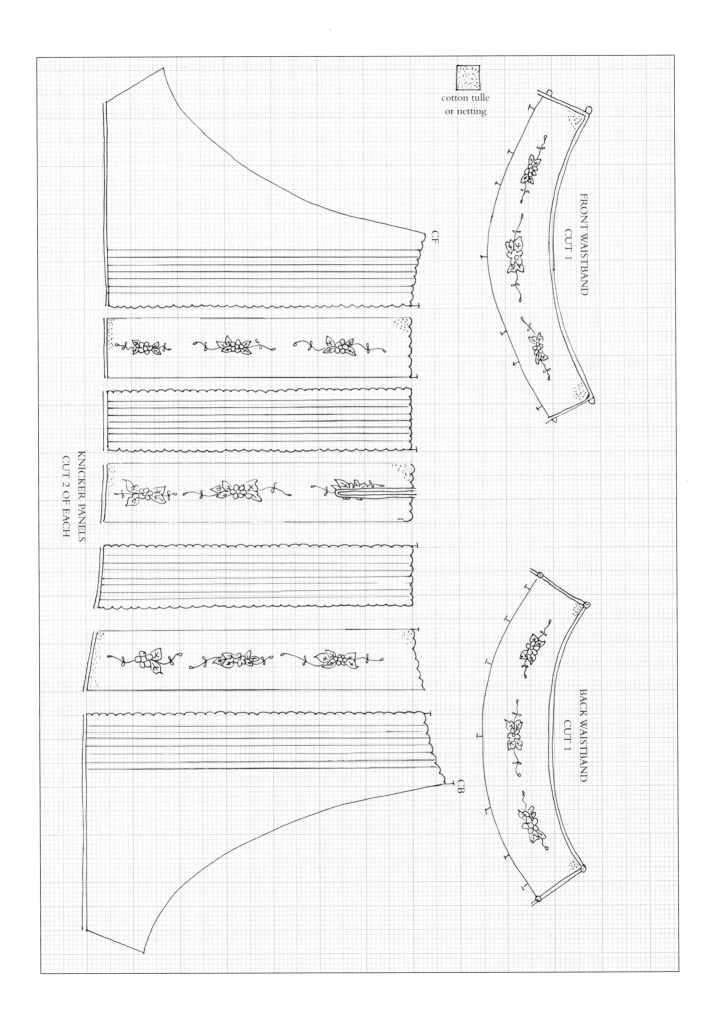

cotton tulle
or netting

FRONT WAISTBAND
CUT 1

BACK WAISTBAND
CUT 1

CF

CB

KNICKER PANELS
CUT 2 OF EACH

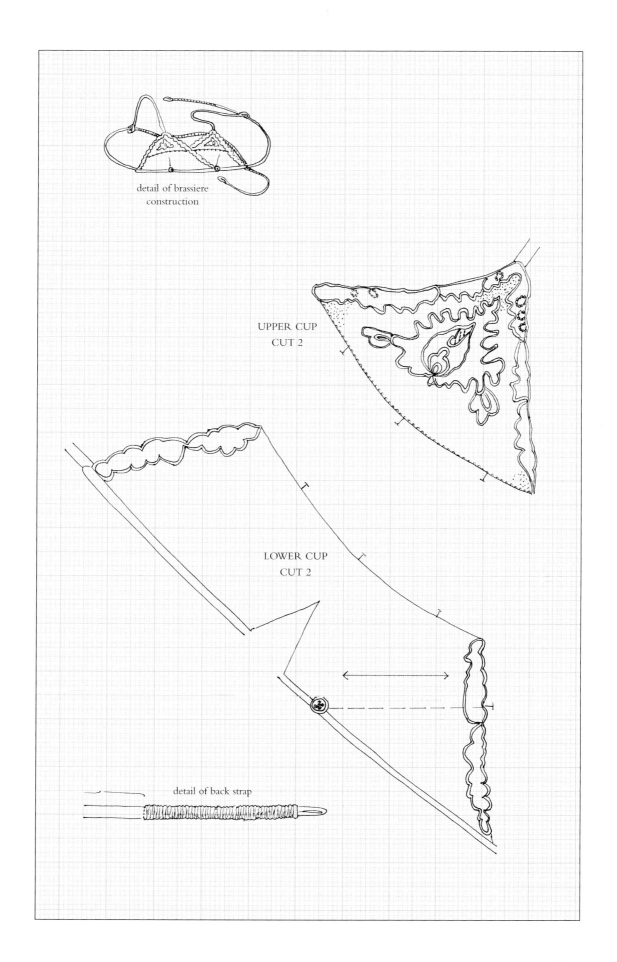

detail of brassiere
construction

UPPER CUP
CUT 2

LOWER CUP
CUT 2

detail of back strap

Patent Brassiere, 1920s

This brassiere, made of cotton or possibly a linen mix, opens at the center front of the garment with small buttons and buttonholes. The breasts would have been unsupported and possibly flattened—ideal for the desired silhouette of the time.

I have included this garment for its patented unusual tightening method; nine laces on either side run through a set of nine eyelets and converge into one lace. By pulling the laces and tying them at the front the garment measurement could be reduced by 3½in (9cm) over the bust and the waist. The lacing system is unusual but it is not unique; I have seen it on the back of 19th-century men's drawers.

Symington patented this lacing method. There were better-designed bandeaus to flatten the bust; if this closure system was used in conjunction with a boned bodice I think it would have been effective, but the substance of this garment is not rigid enough to effectively suppress a body, and the only two bones in it are slender wands in the center back. I think this is probably a nursing brassiere, which would be worn while the mother's figure gradually returned.

Left and right: Front and side views of this 1920s garment show the unusual lacing method that enable the wearer to tighten and fasten at the front.

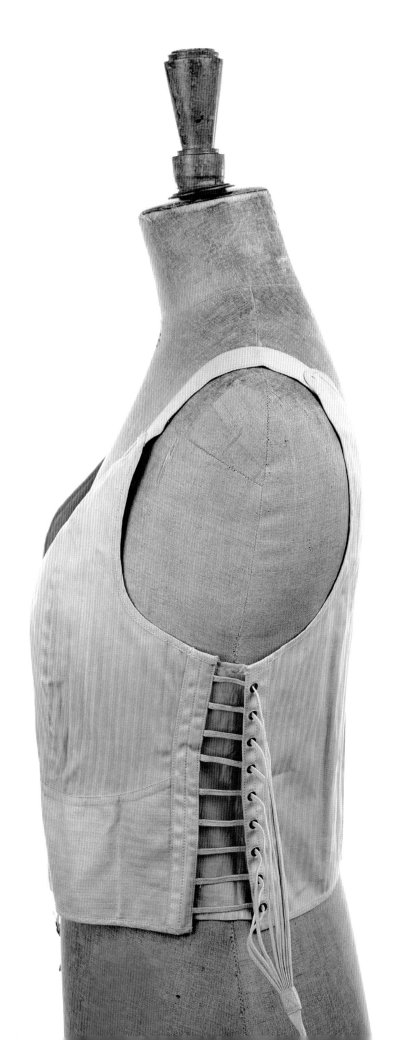

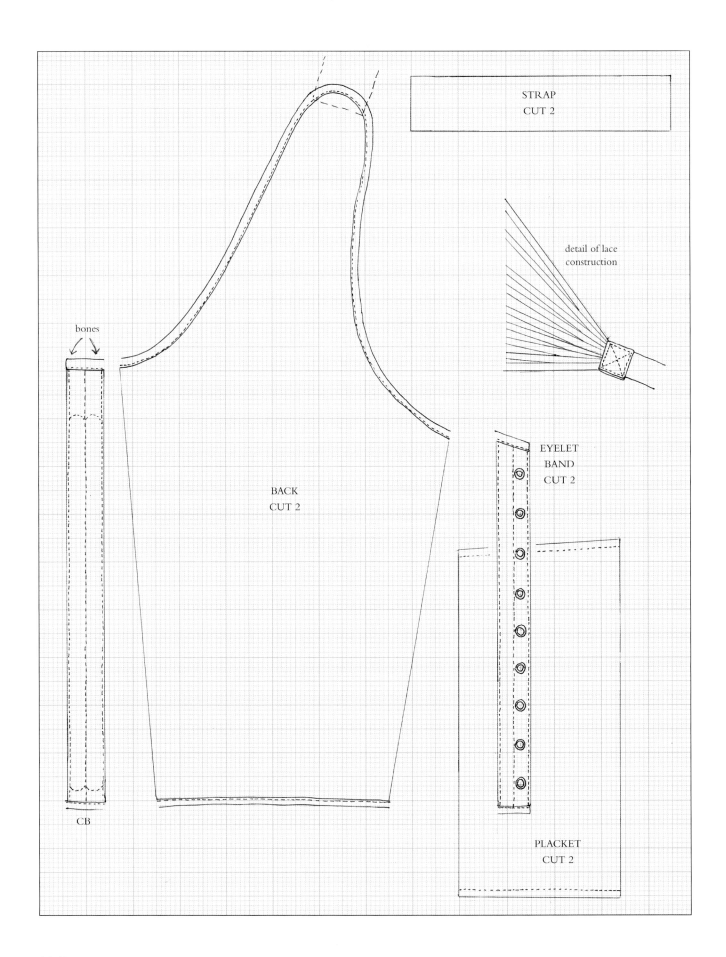

STRAP
CUT 2

detail of lace
construction

bones

BACK
CUT 2

EYELET
BAND
CUT 2

CB

PLACKET
CUT 2

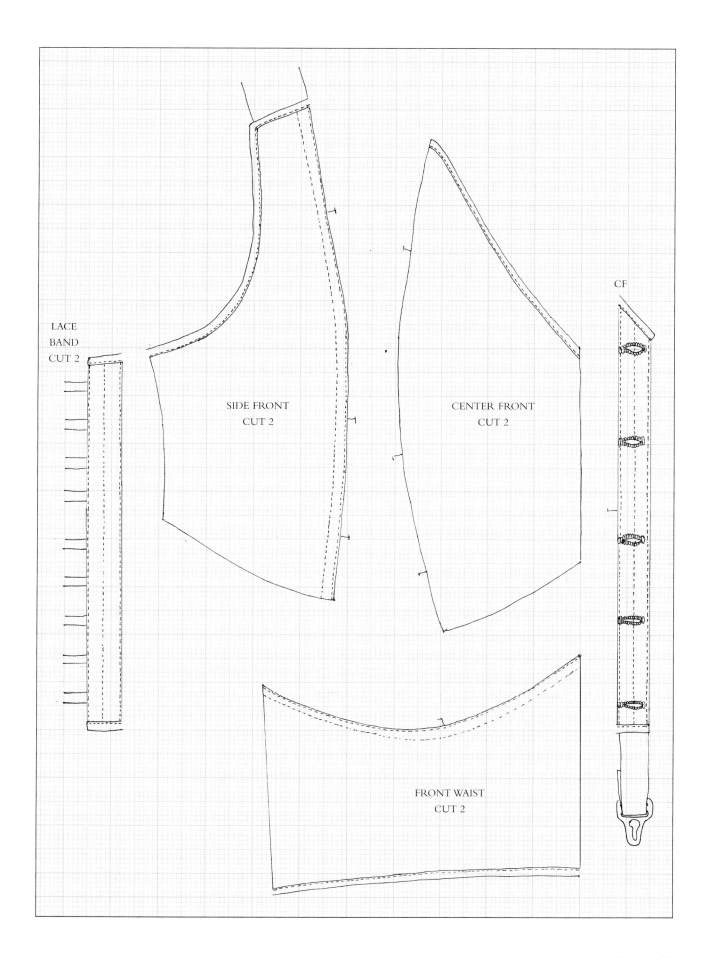

LACE
BAND
CUT 2

SIDE FRONT
CUT 2

CENTER FRONT
CUT 2

CF

FRONT WAIST

CUT 2

Bandeau Brassiere, 1920–30

This garment created the desired shape during the early part of 1920s for the woman who, unfortunately for her at that time in terms of fashion, had a bosom. The bandeau allowed the bosom to find its own level and then gently smoothed it out.

There are three rows of horizontal spiral boning. As it was very unusual to bone any corset or brassiere horizontally, it may be that the boning is decorative rather than practical.

This simple bandeau would give a fluid shape, which was just what was wanted to create the almost boyish figure of that time. It is made of tea-rose colored courtil, with a hook-and-bar side fastening and elastic gussets at the waist edge. At the center front a small elastic tab with a receiver allows the wear to attach the bodice to the lower garments to prevent the bandeau rising up.

The label says "Royal seal" "ARKAY" and it is a Symington's garment; it has satin twill ribbon shoulder straps with no means of adjusting them, except by using needle and thread.

To modern eyes this bandeau is strangely shapeless, but it captures the essence of the period—no frills or flounces, so that the garment worn over it would glide effortlessly on—and it is practical yet attractive in its austerity and utility. Sturdily made, it would last and withstand many launderings. Obviously it is a garment designed for comfort rather than seduction.

Right: This brassiere was designed to smooth out curves and produce a flattened shape.

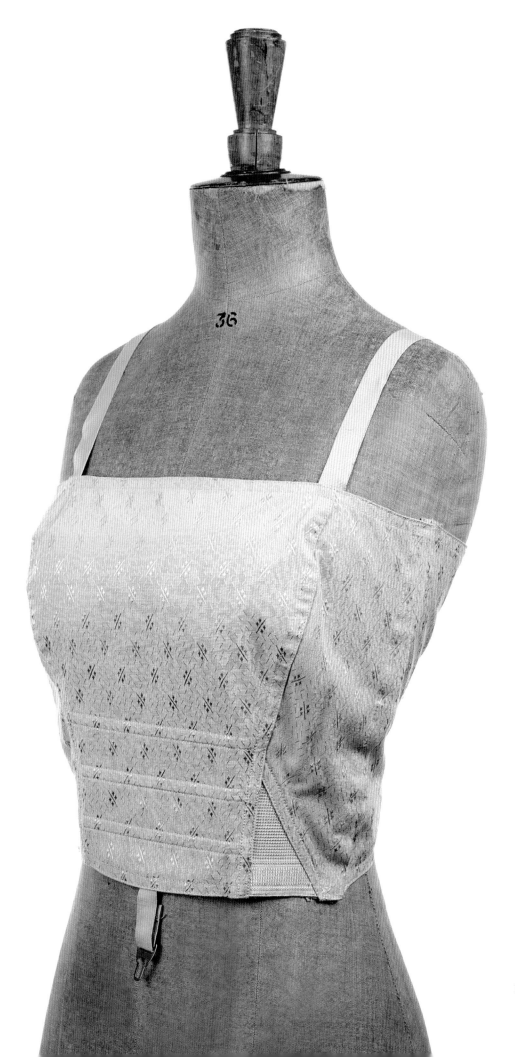

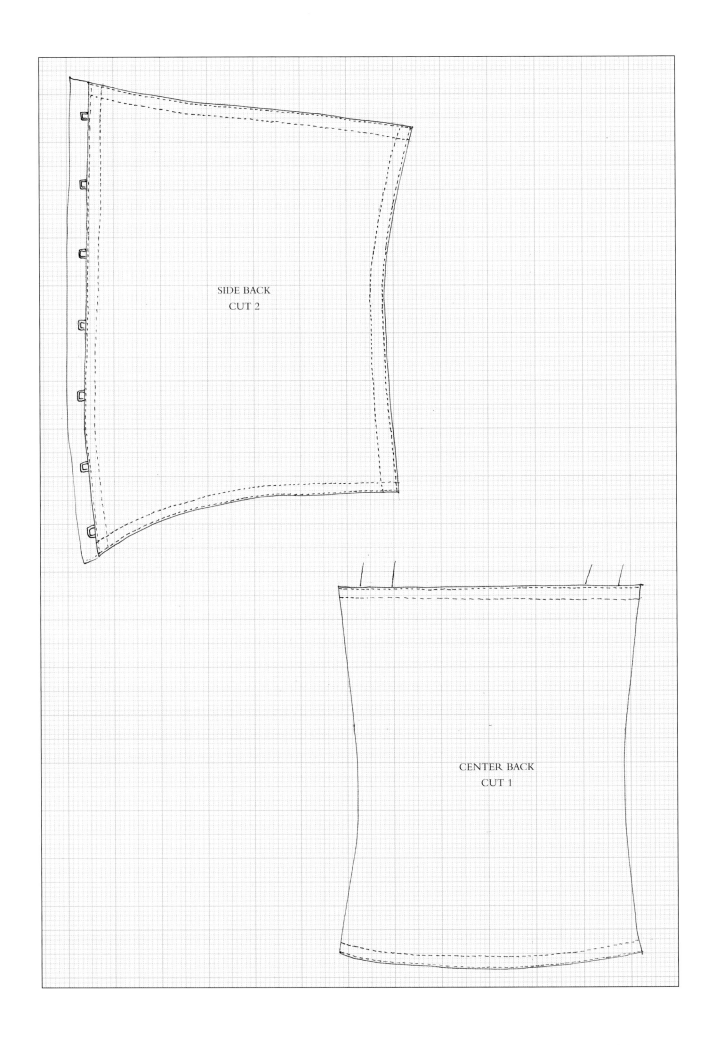

SIDE BACK
CUT 2

CENTER BACK
CUT 1

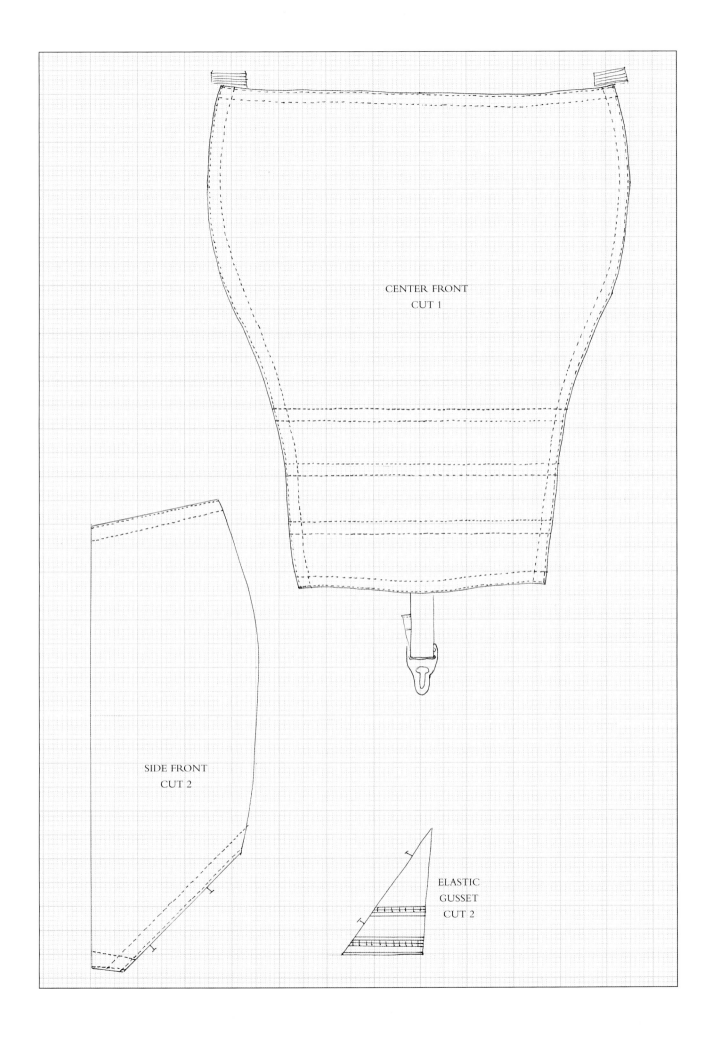

CENTER FRONT
CUT 1

SIDE FRONT
CUT 2

ELASTIC
GUSSET
CUT 2

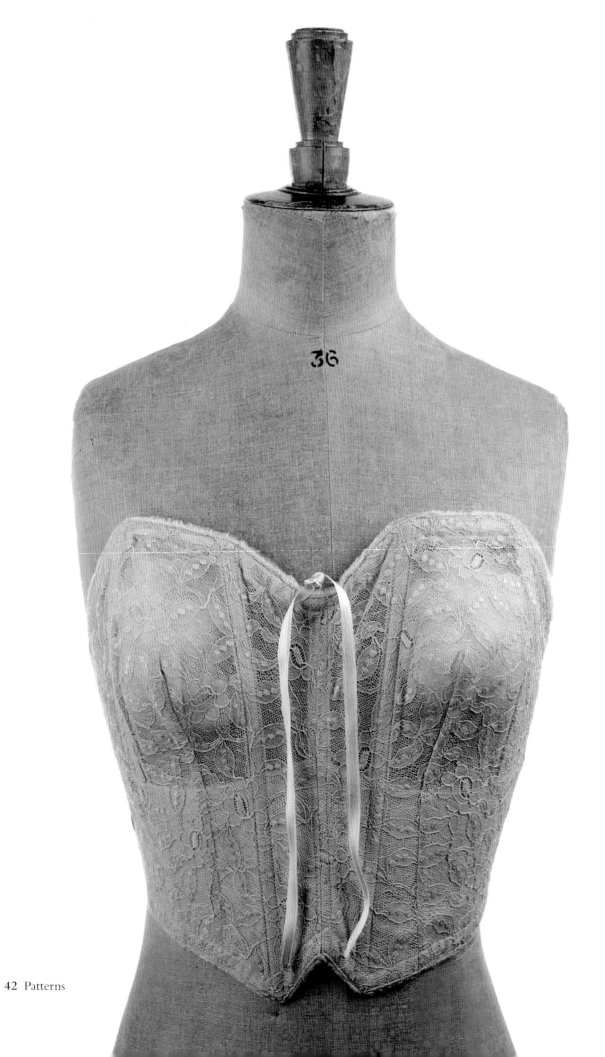

Strapless Brassiere, 1930–7

The ribbon plush lined edges to this garment are partly for comfort and partly decoration. The attention to detail here was to encourage the client to purchase; everything Symington's sold had an underlying practical purpose to support and to protect, so when a client in 1937 was looking to buy a backless basque to wear under an evening dress or sun dress, if the supportive nature of the garment was disguised by pretty lace and satin in a warm, soft color such as tea rose, then the client is tempted because it is so pretty. Very few people would see an undergarment in the 1930s; a maid if you had one, female family members, and possibly one's husband, so the extreme prettiness of these garments was purely to attract the purchaser's eye.

This garment has light, flat, steel boning, the lace fabric is mounted on strong cotton tulle or netting and it has small elastic gussets. It is clearly a pre-war brassiere; World War II brought many restrictions on the production of garments, with shortages and controls that would not be lifted for 14 years.

The ribbon ties seen on the outside of this garment can be used to draw the garment's upper edge closer to the body and then be tucked in out of sight.

Left: A pretty 1930s long-line brassiere. The highly decorative detail suggests it is a pre-war garment, designed before the production restrictions of World War II.

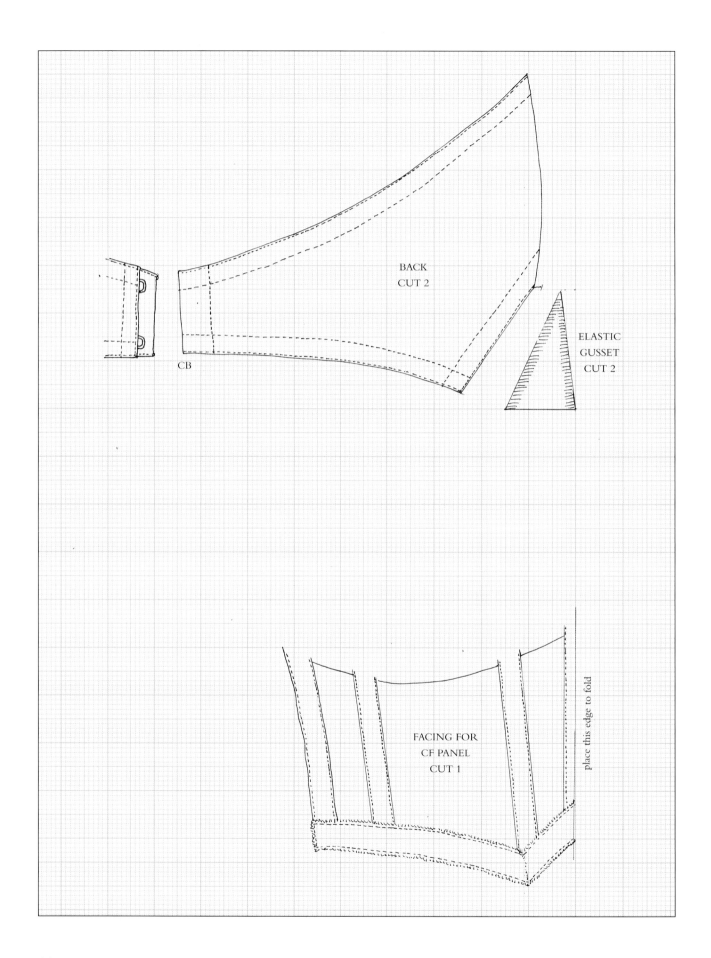

BACK
CUT 2

CB

ELASTIC
GUSSET
CUT 2

FACING FOR
CF PANEL
CUT 1

place this edge to fold

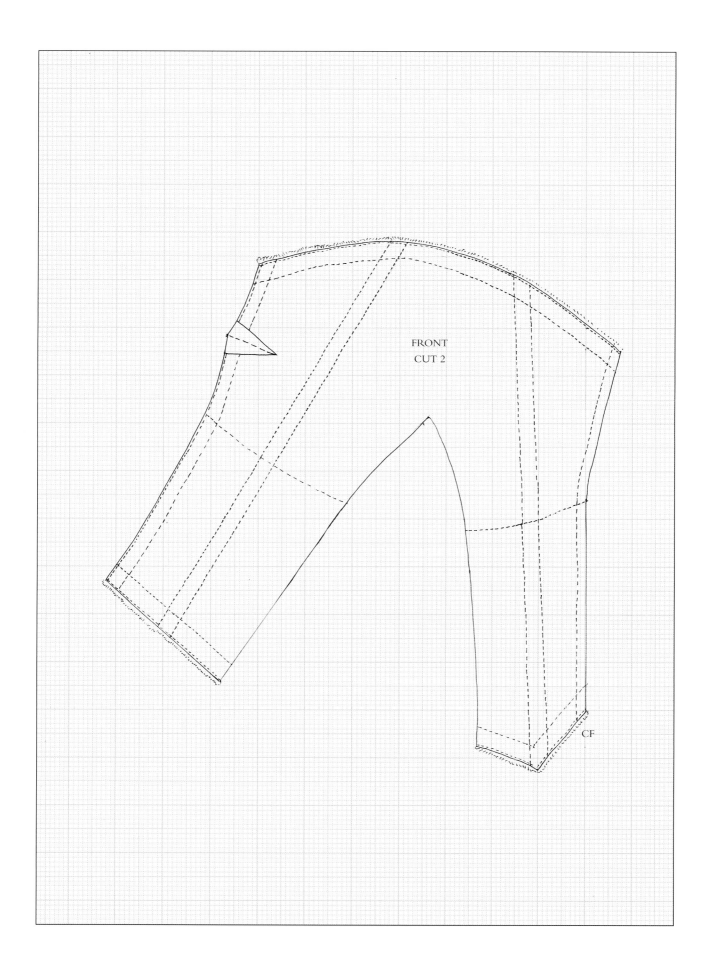

FRONT
CUT 2

CF

Blue Silk Slip, 1930s

From the early 1920s waist slips disappeared and princess slips became fashionable. These slips were made of silk crêpe de Chine, soft silk satin, and were non see-through, allowing dresses to glide over them. In some cases they were designed as under-dresses for sheer voile and chiffon top-dresses. Dresses of the early 1920s may have been square cut and a little shapeless but the princess slips underneath often had waists and clung to the body.

This slip possibly dates from the early 1930s as it is long and lean, and it would have been suitable under a bias-cut dress allowing a flowing silhouette. All of its seams are machine-stitched French seams except the decorative bust-line seam, which is faggoted by hand. The raw edges inside the slip are finished off with hand-sewn blanket stitch in silk. The top and hem edges of the slip are finished with a bias fabric binding in the same silk as the garment, attached by machine and hand finished at ¼in (5mm) wide. The straps have also been constructed in crêpe de Chine. The decoration in the front panel is drawn thread work and eyelet work, again sewn by hand. It is simple and stylish, with an Art Deco look to it.

This would have been a figure-hugging garment as it has a side closure with four tiny hooks, which are buttonhole stitched on, and four hand-worked loops. There is no label in this garment; it could be homemade but this is unlikely.

It is possible to find examples of these slips at vintage fairs as they seem to survive better than the dresses that were worn over them.

Left: This princess slip from the 1930s would have been worn underneath a bias-cut dress.

Below: Careful drawn thread and eyelet embroidery on the front panel was worked by hand.

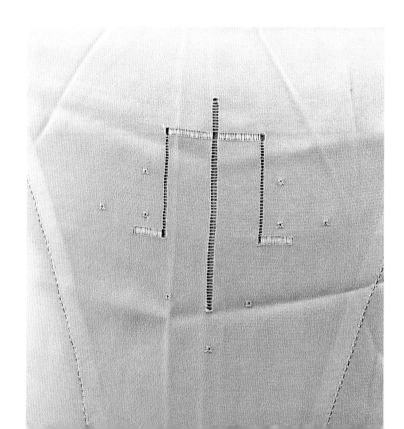

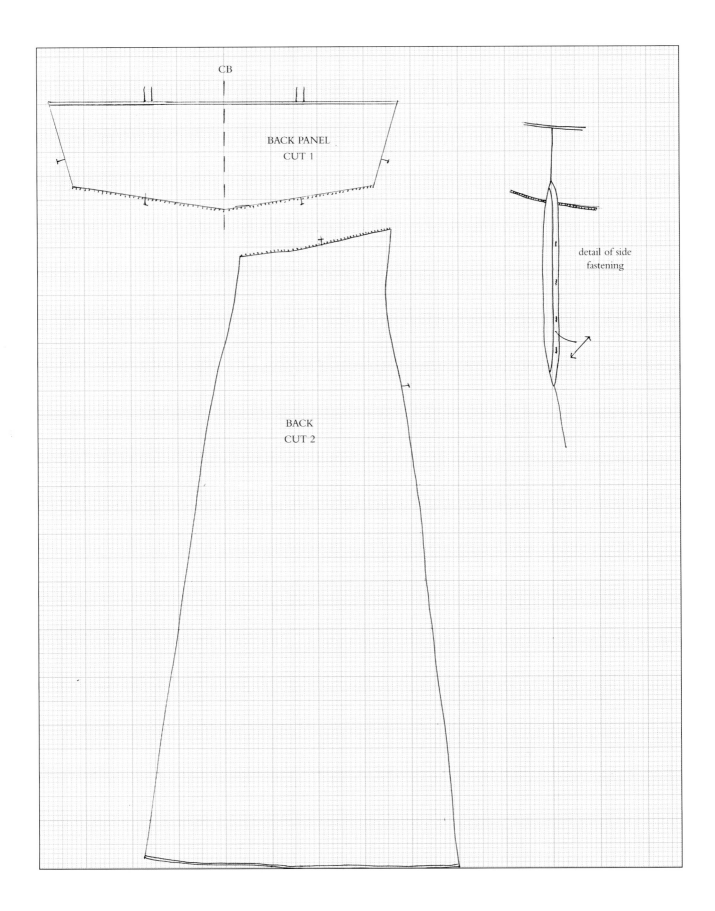

CB

BACK PANEL
CUT 1

BACK
CUT 2

detail of side
fastening

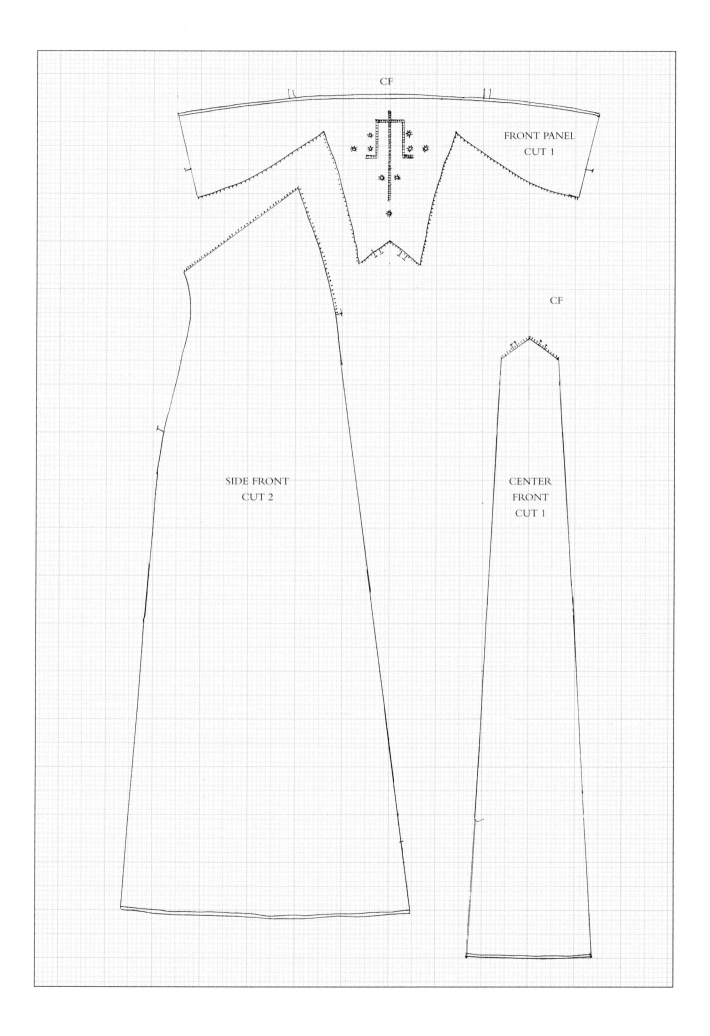

CF

FRONT PANEL
CUT 1

CF

SIDE FRONT
CUT 2

CENTER
FRONT
CUT 1

50 Patterns

Girdle, 1932

From the end of World War II, undergarments—particularly for the younger woman—altered dramatically from those worn at the turn of the 20th century. No longer were they white, but soft, exciting colors, and they were more likely to be in washable, lighter-weight silks. By this time, the young thing of the 1920s and 30s was probably wearing a bra, and her directoire knickers or drawers could have shortened in all senses to "panties," which is where the girdle came in.

In the 1920s women wanted flattened bosoms and narrow hips. To achieve the desired shape dieting was popular, along with foundation garments such as girdles.

This is a Symington's girdle; tea rose in color, made of courtil, boned with spiral wires (whalebone was hardly used by this time), with a split-busk fastening at the center front and a laced center back. This is a girdle for a woman who is determined to have the shape she wants, although strangely the label in this girdle states "designed for waist 24in (60cm)" and the hip measurement is about 32in (80cm); it is hard to imagine anyone with those slim measurements needing such determined corseting.

By now elastic was widely used, so presumably the purchaser could have found a more comfortable way to achieve her desired shape than wires and lacing.

Far left: Girdles like this one were used to create the fashionable flattened silhouette of the 1930s.

Left: The garment could be tightened using the lacing at the back.

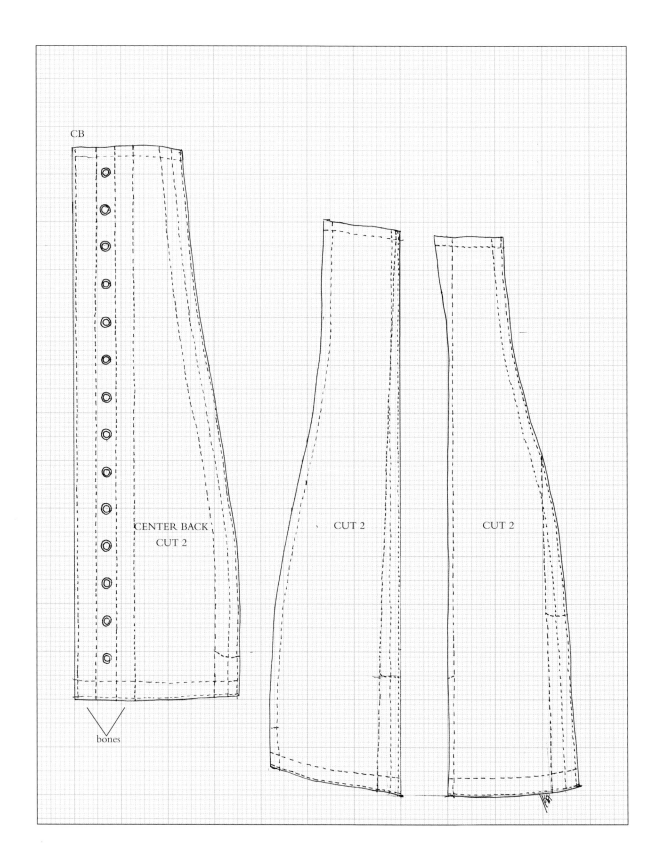

CB

CENTER BACK
CUT 2

bones

CUT 2

CUT 2

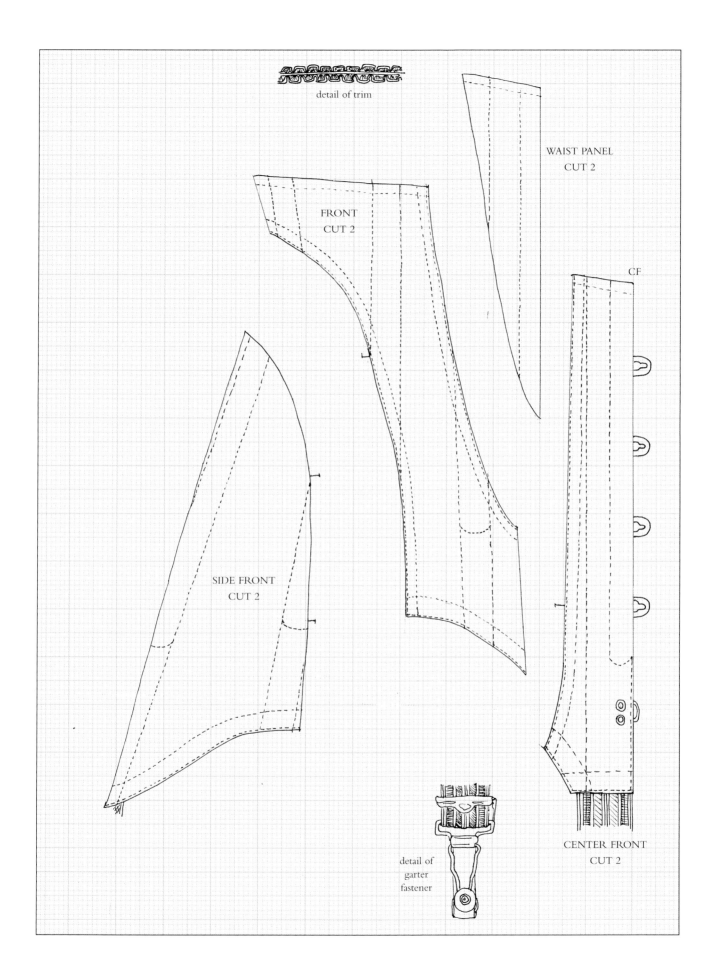

detail of trim

WAIST PANEL
CUT 2

FRONT
CUT 2

CF

SIDE FRONT
CUT 2

detail of
garter
fastener

CENTER FRONT
CUT 2

Maternity Girdle, 1940s

This Symington's maternity girdle is printed with an AVRO label and the Utility mark. At the height of World War II in 1941 the British Board of Trade introduced a scheme for manufactured goods that dictated the amount or type of fabric and decoration that was permitted, and also how long could be spent constructing items. All garments made under this scheme bore the Utility mark, like the one shown on this garment. Restrictions were not lifted until 1952. The Utility mark on this maternity girdle is perhaps surprising given its 56 metal eyelets, four large metal suspenders, and a substantial hook-and-eye fastening.

The Symington AVRO brand was introduced in 1923, named after a friend of the Symington family, A.V. Roe (1877–1970), who was responsible for developing the successful AVRO fighter plane of World War I. Roe was the first Briton to fly an all-British plane and was founder of the AVRO aircraft firm. By 1929 his firm had built 10,000 planes, mainly for the British Royal Air Force. Over the years Symington's chose a variety of names for the garments they manufactured. Possibly the name AVRO was selected because the garments had superstructures, as did planes, and because AVRO was a name that people connected with quality, reliability and the cutting edge of technology, which Symington's wanted to associate that with their garments.

This girdle fits the description of one produced by Symington's in 1935: "Shaped to fit over the abdomen there are three small bones, two at the base and one at the top." The channels are there, but have never been boned in this garment; possibly the three small bones were sacrificed in the war effort.

The tea-rose colored courtil girdle has two panels of lacing as well as a side front fastening of hooks and eyes and, despite the elastic front panel, this is a garment that is designed to constrict.

Left: A maternity garment like this one from the 1940s would be frowned upon today because it is so constricting.

Below: Label showing the utility mark (center) stamped on the garment.

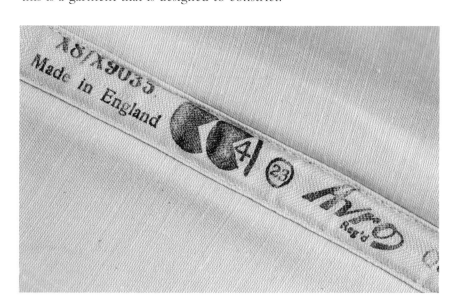

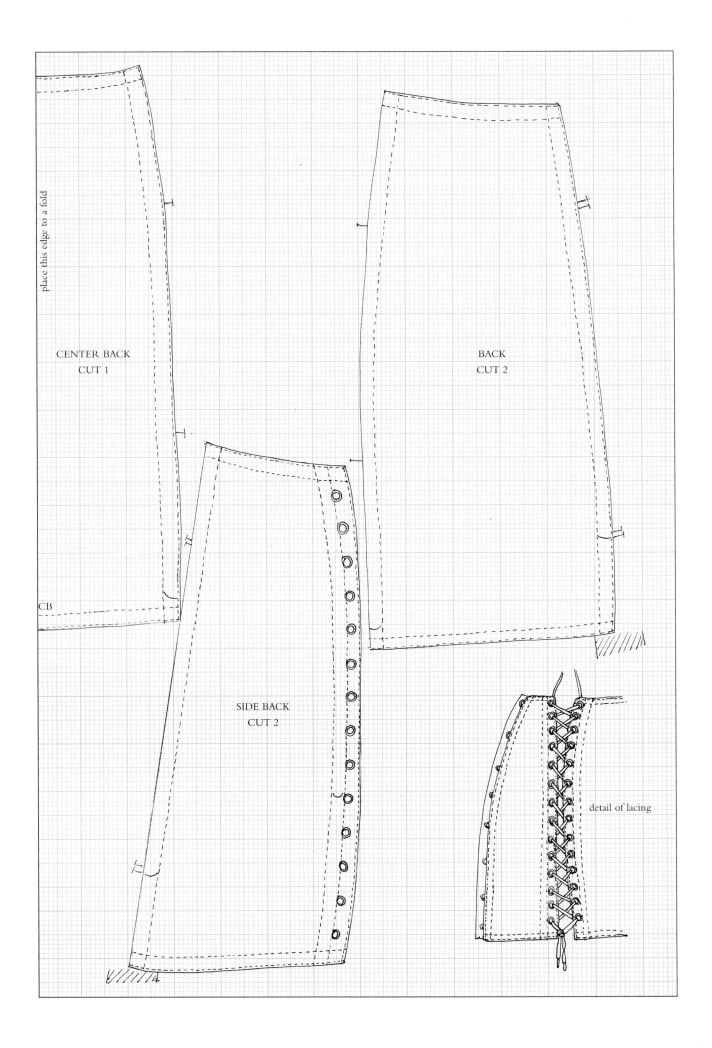

place this edge to a fold

CENTER BACK
CUT 1

CB

BACK
CUT 2

SIDE BACK
CUT 2

detail of lacing

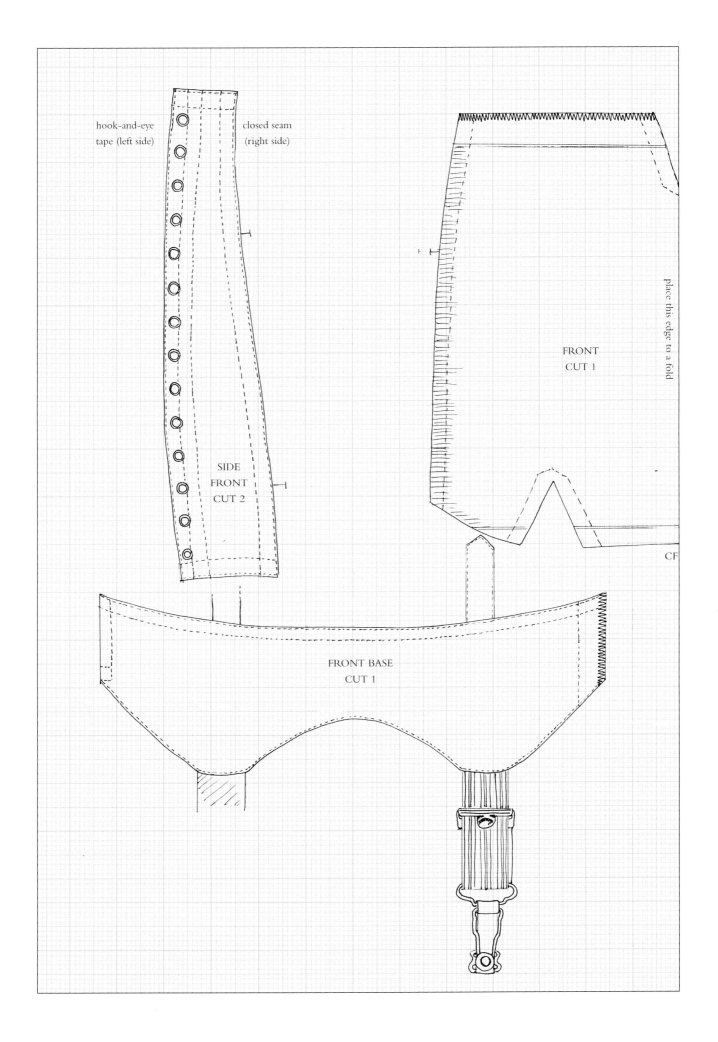

hook-and-eye
tape (left side)

closed seam
(right side)

FRONT
CUT 1

place this edge to a fold

SIDE
FRONT
CUT 2

CF

FRONT BASE
CUT 1

Linen Knickers, 1940s

These are dressmaker-made knickers from around 1940; the few seams are machine stitched and then hand felled down with the neatest, minute hand stitches 28:1in (28:2.5cm). The leg of the knickers would extend 3in (8cm) down the wearer's leg where it is caught in with eight cord elastic. The elastic was contrived to be removable for laundering with a hand-sewn loop and a flat linen button; the attention to detail is quite humbling.

The simple but useful pattern for these knickers is not vastly different to that for the combinations shown at the beginning of this book (see page 22) and similar patterns can be found in *The Work Woman's Guide*, first published in 1838 (see Further Reading, page 124).

These knickers are made of fine linen with a plaid pattern woven in, which indicates that they may have been over-knickers. There is also a small pocket on the front. There is a lovely plain dress that goes with them, the sort you could imagine being used for cycling or hiking in the summer.

Linen was always popular for underwear until it was succeeded by cotton, wool, and then silk. Linen is stronger wet than dry, which allows it to be vigorously washed. It is cool and crisp in summer.

Below: Linen knickers from the 1940s, with removable elastic for washing.

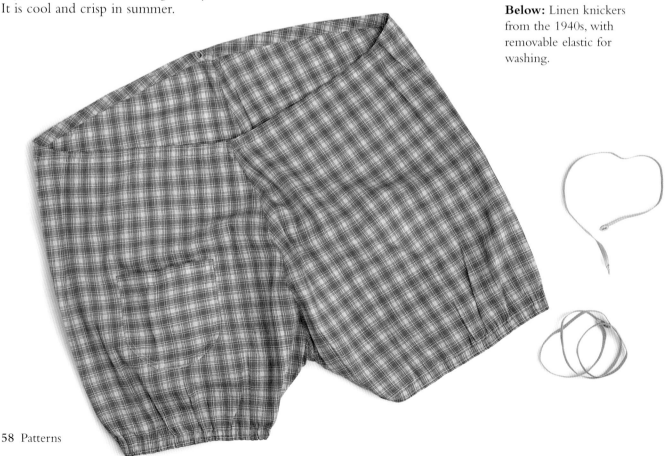

Satin Suspender Knickers, 1969

In contrast to the linen knickers shown opposite, these satin suspender knickers cannot have been cool and crisp to wear. These are made of nylon and Lycra satin jacquard, with detachable suspenders. These were detachable for two reasons: firstly for washing; and secondly because by now tights were available in department stores, which was a boon to the mini dress wearers of 1969.

The knickers are trimmed with a narrow band of soft finished elastic around each leg for a comfortable fit and over-trimmed with a stretch lace. They would have supported a trim figure, but would have had little impact on a more generous one.

By this date there had been complete change in what was worn as underwear. There is little or no restriction, man-made fabrics and lace are used, items are easy to put on and wash (with no need for maids for dressing or laundering), but still there is attention to detail in color and finish for a garment very few people would see. As with the underwear of the 1880s the garments are pretty and colorful to seduce the buyer.

Right: These knickers from 1969 have a fastening for suspenders, although tights were available in department stores by this time.

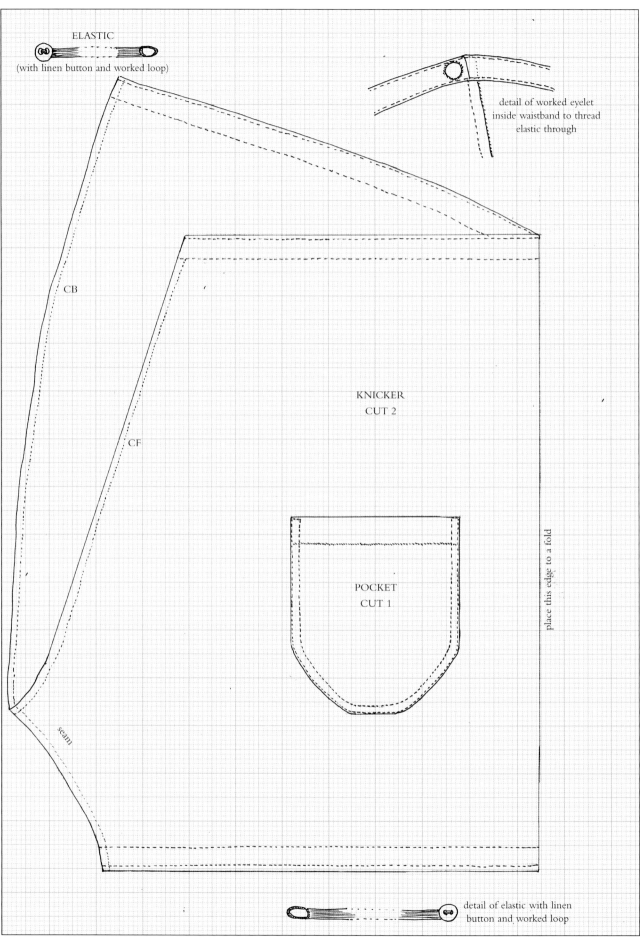

ELASTIC

(with linen button and worked loop)

detail of worked eyelet
inside waistband to thread
elastic through

CB

CF

KNICKER
CUT 2

place this edge to a fold

POCKET
CUT 1

seam

detail of elastic with linen
button and worked loop

Linen Knickers

Satin Suspender Knickers

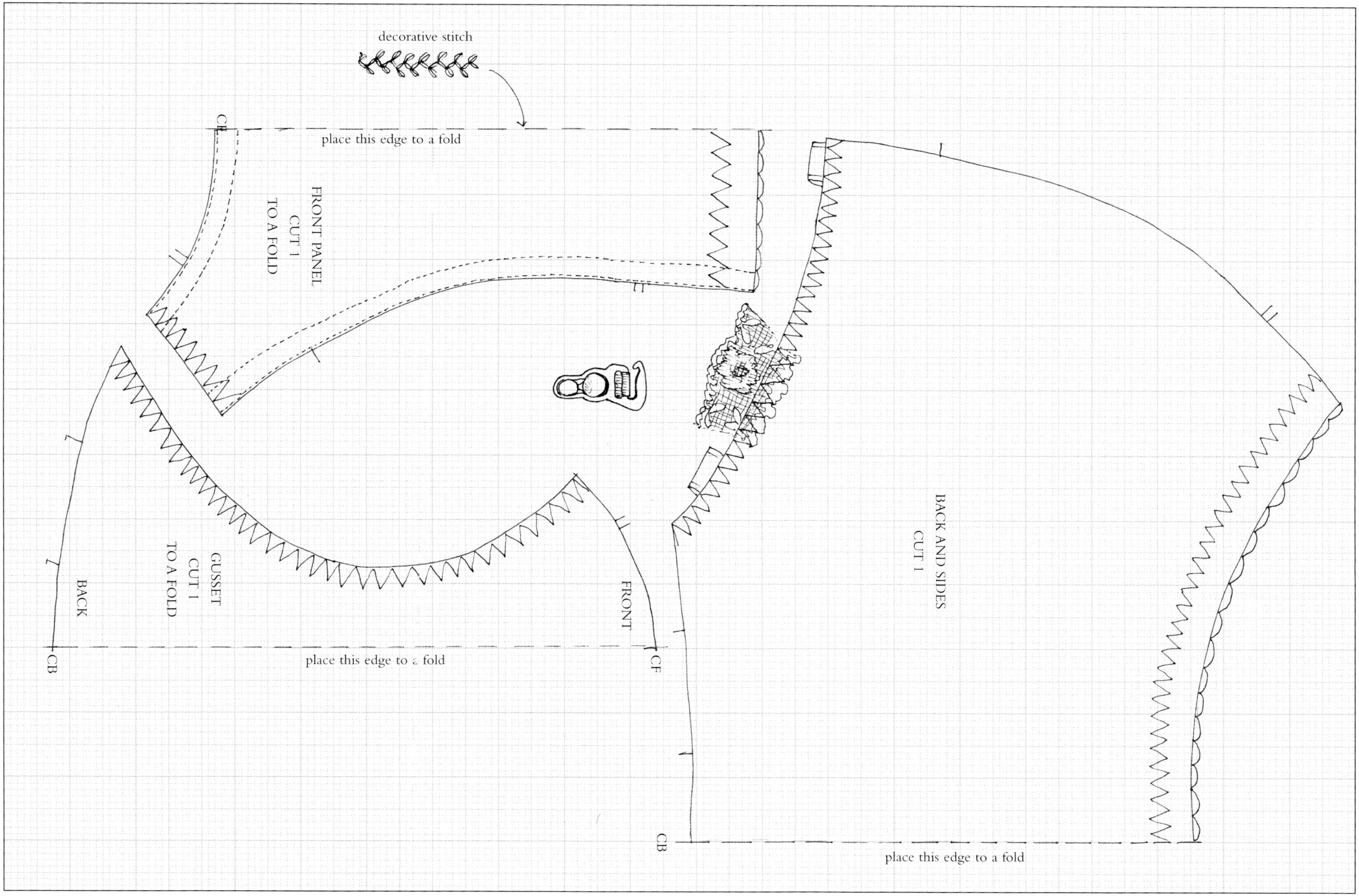

BACK AND SIDES
CUT 1

place this edge to a fold

CF

CB

FRONT

decorative stitch

place this edge to a fold

FRONT PANEL
CUT 1
TO A FOLD

CF

place this edge to a fold

GUSSET
CUT 1
TO A FOLD

BACK

CB

White Satin Girdle, 1930s

Model No. B446F is a neat, undecorated girdle. It was also available in tea-rose color (as stated on the attached label), which means it would have to have been made after 1932, as this was when Symington's started using the tea-rose color. It has no Utility mark, so must have been made before the restrictions on garment production were introduced during World War II (see page 55 for more information).

It has two metal bones encased in cardboard in the boning channels on the front panel, and has side panels of woven elastic, which look very comfortable. This garment has a waist of 23in (58cm) and hips of 32in (80cm), so it is a lightweight girdle for holding up the stockings of a lightweight woman. It fastens at the side front with hook-and-eye tape, is made of satin-faced coutil, and has four substantial suspenders.

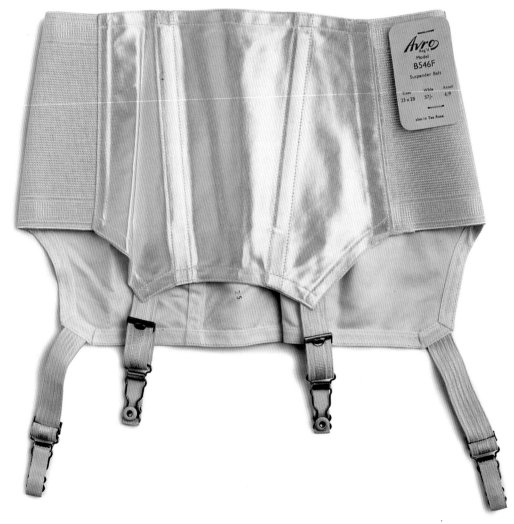

Below: A neat and practical girdle used for holding up stockings in the 1940s.

Tea-rose Garter Belt, 1940s

Garters for both men and women had been used for centuries to hold stockings in place on the leg. Later corsets and girdles took over this role, but by the late 20th century these had fallen out of fashion and garter belts, such as the one shown here, were invented to make wearing stockings more comfortable. Symington first introduced them in 1906 then withdrew them, reintroducing them in the late 1920s, and they proved extremely popular throughout the 1930s.

Many period garter belts incorporate the same fabrics they do today, namely lace and silk. This example from the 1940s is made in a pretty, light pink satin and is a simple, four-attachment garter belt. Two attachments on each side connect to the stockings; one in the front of the leg and one in the back. This arrangement was not thought as secure and didn't function as well as the six-attachment version.

It is made using satin-faced coutil, this time in the delightful tea-rose color, with fine lace edging in peach and a little rose-and-leaf embellishment at its center front. Rubber and elastic suspenders and a little light boning on the center front panel are enough to be uncomfortable but not strong enough to correct any faults in the figure.

Below: Garter belts like this one from the 1940s replaced garters as the fashionable way to hold stockings in place.

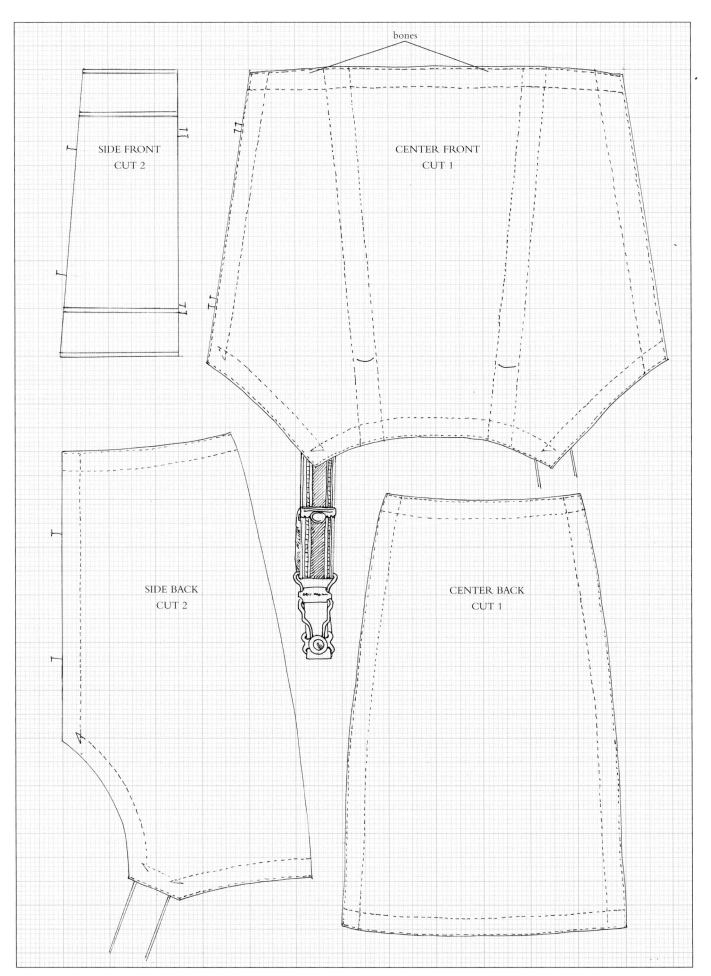

bones

SIDE FRONT
CUT 2

CENTER FRONT
CUT 1

SIDE BACK
CUT 2

CENTER BACK
CUT 1

White Satin Girdle

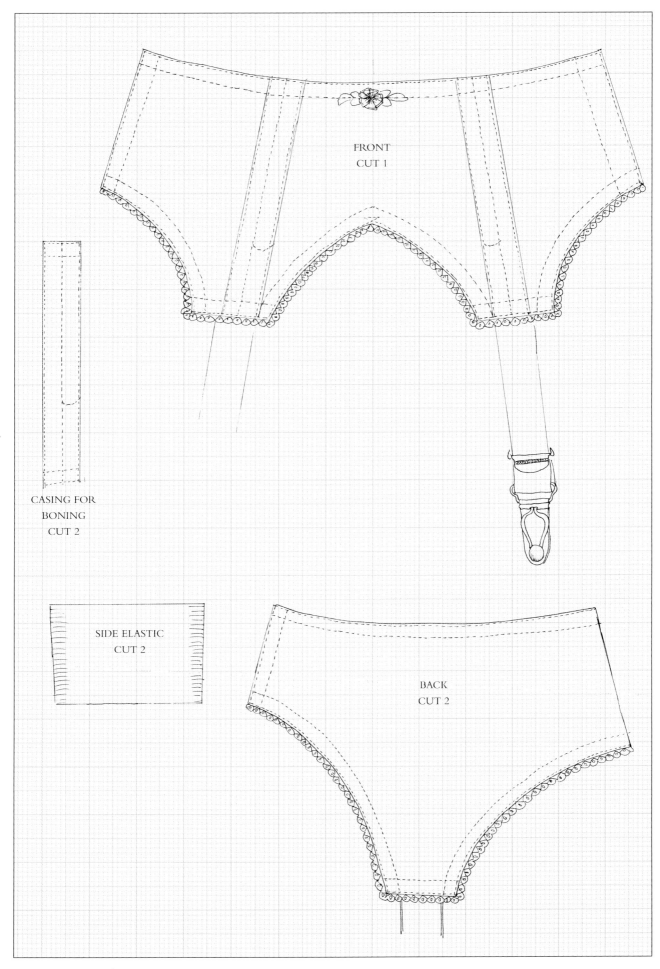

FRONT
CUT 1

CASING FOR
BONING
CUT 2

SIDE ELASTIC
CUT 2

BACK
CUT 2

Tea-rose Garter Belt

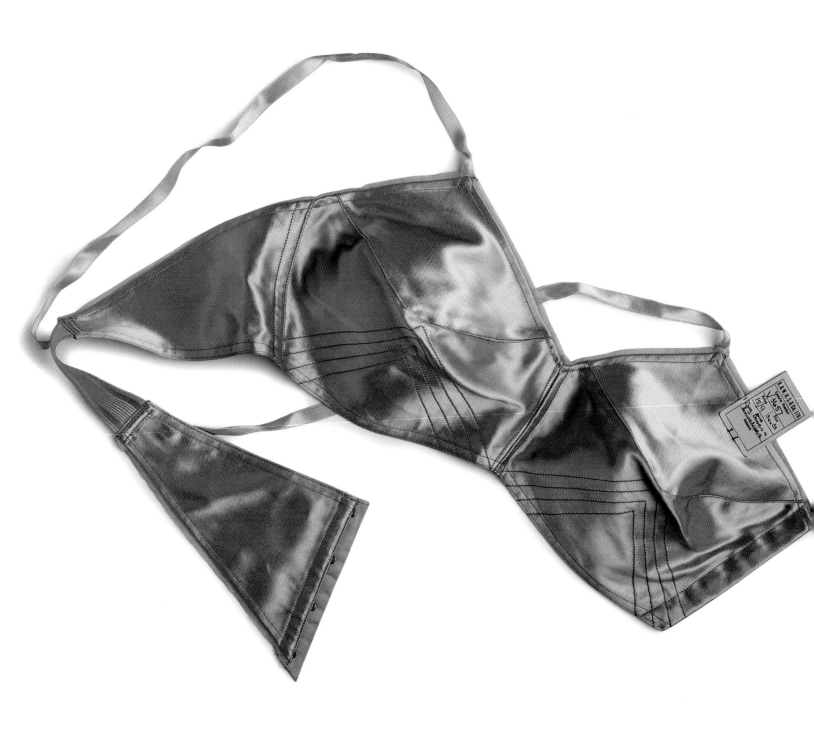

Satin Bra, 1937 and Utility Brassiere, 1940s

The satin bra shown opposite is made of tea-rose colored satin-faced coutil with an inner lining of fine cotton or linen; all edges have been bias bound and double stitched. There is a top edge of fine tulle or netting, there are no bones and no means of altering the bra strap; it has elastic across the center back and a side front fastening of tea-rose colored hook-and-eye tape. It has a stitched pattern under the bust, has no label and it has never been worn.

By contrast, its plainer cousin shown below, also made of silk and lined in cotton, has a label stating it was made by ADLIS and DECOLET. It has no lace, two very narrow bands of elastic at the back and two hooks and eyes; unsurprisingly it has a Utility label (see page 55). This bra has a small top-stitched insert under the bust, slightly stiffened. It looks like it would have given moral rather than actual support.

One of the aims of the Utility system was to cut down production time, but there is a lot of construction required in this garment, probably equal to that of the satin non-Utility bra.

Left and below: These pre-war and post-war brassieres demonstrate the effects of the Utility system brought in during World War II.

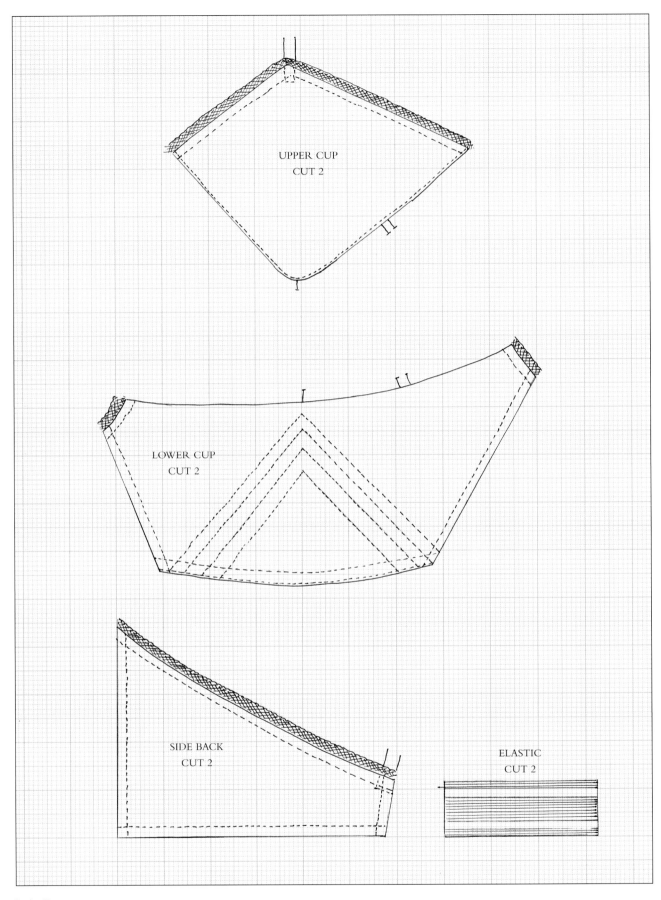

UPPER CUP
CUT 2

LOWER CUP
CUT 2

SIDE BACK
CUT 2

ELASTIC
CUT 2

Satin Bra

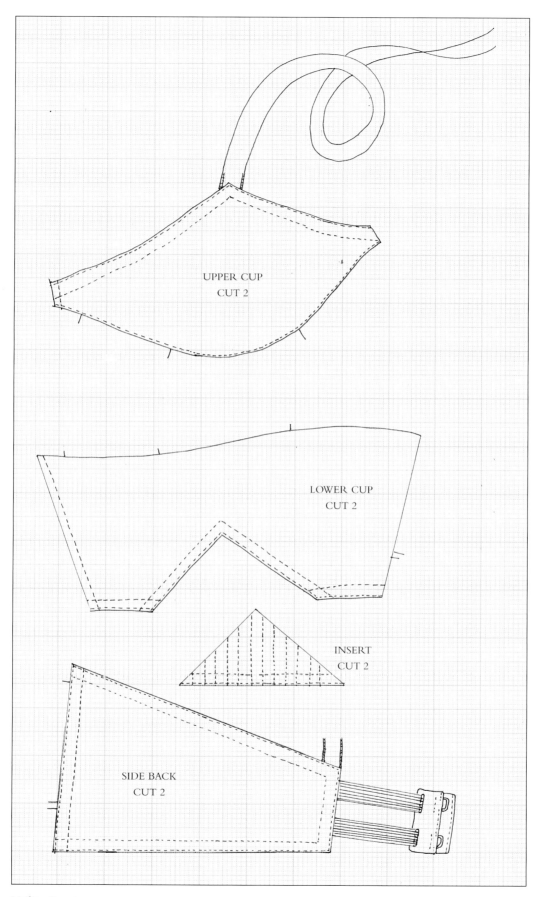

UPPER CUP
CUT 2

LOWER CUP
CUT 2

INSERT
CUT 2

SIDE BACK
CUT 2

Utility Brassiere

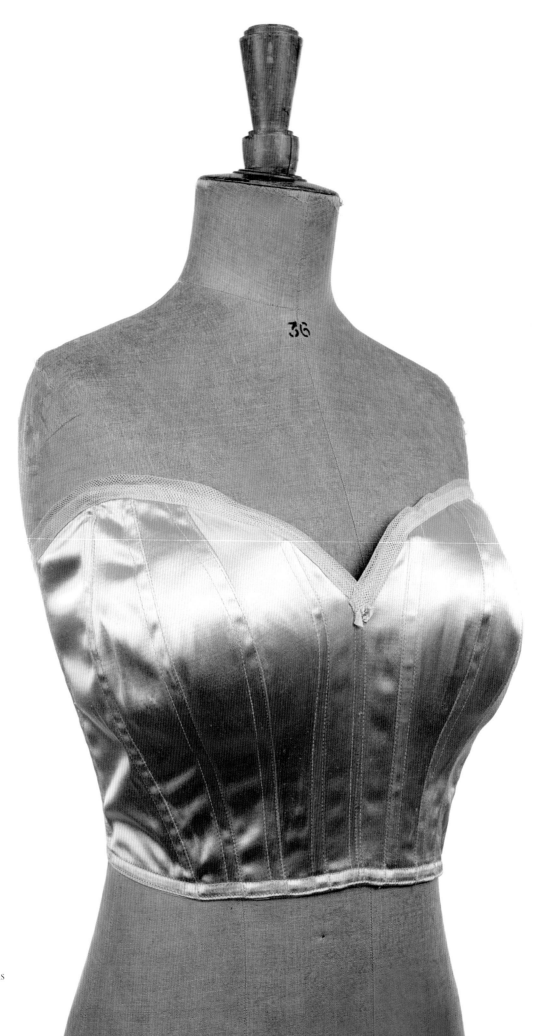

Strapless Brassiere, 1940s

This strapless brassiere was presumably intended for evening wear. It would have fitted a well-endowed woman, as the label states it is for a 40in (102cm) bust.

It is trimmed with a soft tulle or netting trim, pretty enough not to ruin the line of the garment worn over it. A small rose-and-leaf trim at the center front is very similar that on the tea-rose garter belt (see page 63), dated 1940.

It has been recognized that the fashion shapes that emerged after World War II were already embryonic in the late 1930s; if this strapless brassiere was made from nylon it could date from the early 1950s. However, in satin-faced coutil, with extensive elastic panels, matching the 1940s tea-rose garter belt in every way, it is most likely that it dates from around 1940.

It has six panels at the front; each seam has a bone casing but only half of them are filled with supple ¼in (5mm) flat steel bones. It is a nicely cut shape but is not a very supportive garment.

Left: This 1940s brassiere is a strapless garment designed to fit beneath eveningwear and demonstrates how the post-war fashion shapes of the 1950s were forming over a decade earlier.

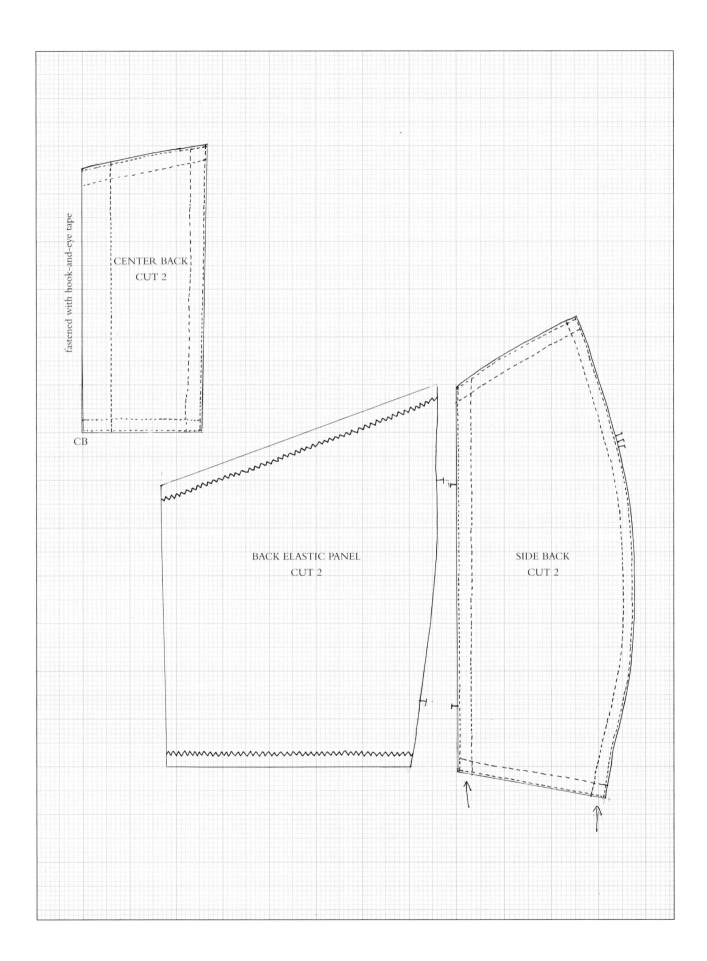

fastened with hook-and-eye tape

CENTER BACK
CUT 2

CB

BACK ELASTIC PANEL
CUT 2

SIDE BACK
CUT 2

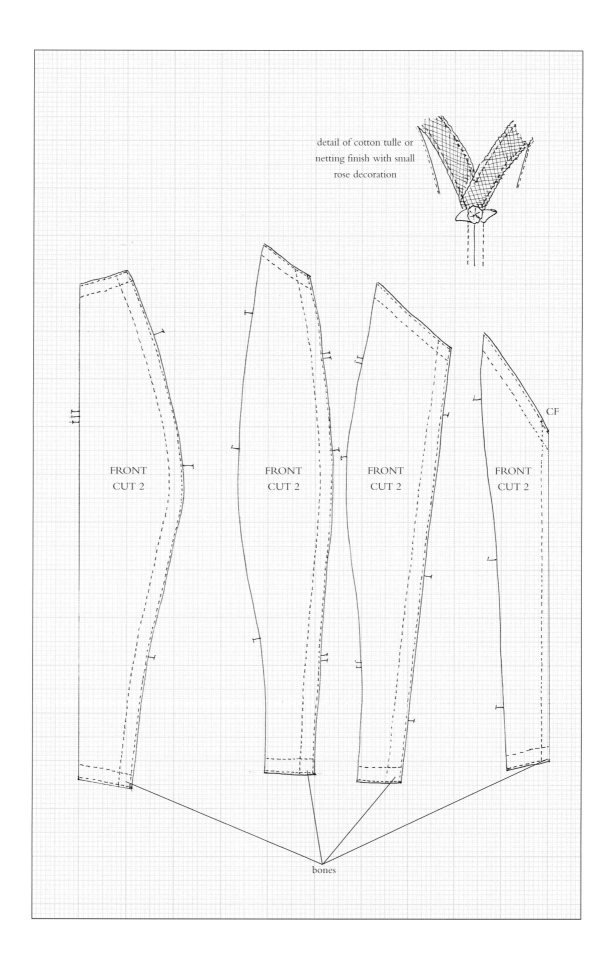

detail of cotton tulle or
netting finish with small
rose decoration

FRONT
CUT 2

FRONT
CUT 2

FRONT
CUT 2

FRONT
CUT 2

CF

bones

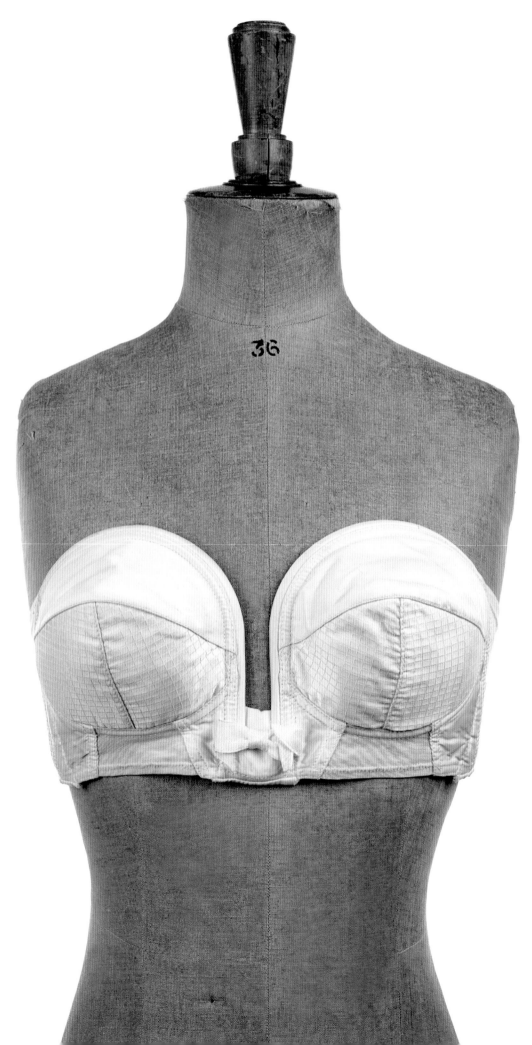

Strapless Brassiere and Waist Cincher, 1950s

This is an Exquisite Form strapless brassiere, donated by Mrs. Margret Cross of Brecon, and worn soon after Dior's "New Look" emerged in 1947. It is very similar to a brassiere produced by Symington's in 1955. Underwear manufacturers were quite happy to adapt profitable lines by their competitors, and once they came up with a successful shape it would remain on their production line as long as there was a market for it. This style may have been available before 1955.

On the label it says B34 and there is an instruction not to iron the cups, which are nearly ¼in (5mm) thick, made of a nylon type fabric, with an outer and inner shell and something quite substantial in between. These are extensive areas of elastic that attempt to hold the garment up.

I have included this brassiere in this book of useful patterns as a curiosity, since the wires are overwires as opposed to the underwires we are familiar with today. Having tried it on someone of the right size it does have a tendency to creep down the torso.

The "New Look" waist cincher was made by Gossard and would have aided the return of a woman's 24–26in (60–65cm) waist after childbirth. Suspenders have been removed, the elastic is perishing and the spiral wire bones are distorted to the wearer's curves. It was obviously a useful garment, probably reasonably costly in its day, made of tea-rose satin-faced coutil, with the remains of plush ribbon on the reverse of the hook-and-eye tape.

A garment like this heralded the new woman of the 1950s, wearing roll-ons, girdles, all-in-one corsets, slips, and garter belts; a woman still trussed up and not to be released or relieved for another 20 years. Society during this time still put pressure on women to be restrained and reshaped by their underwear.

Left and right: This strapless brassiere and waist cincher are characteristic of Dior's "New Look," popular in the 1950s.

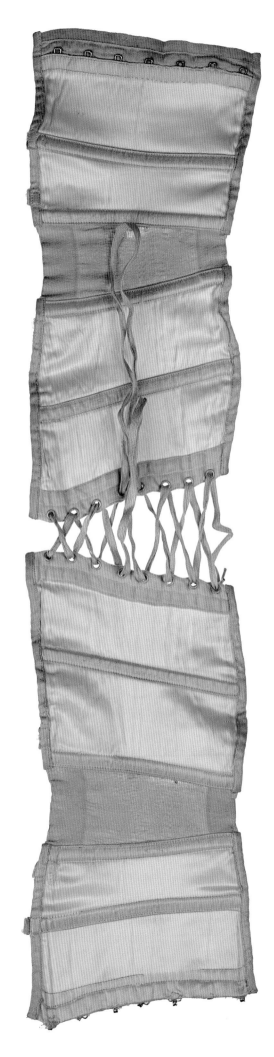

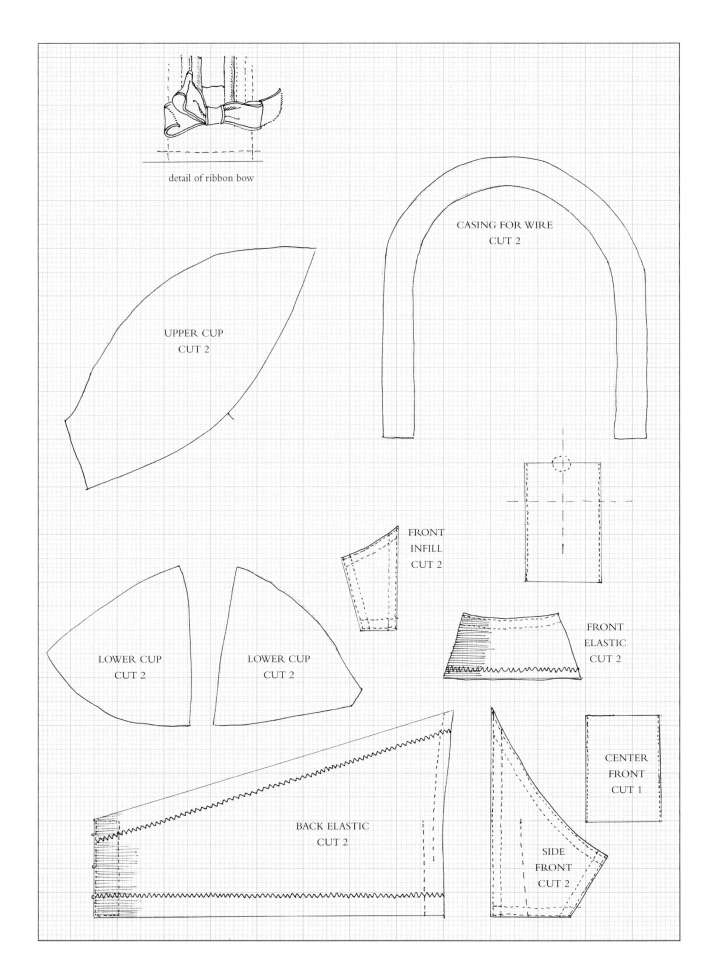

detail of ribbon bow

CASING FOR WIRE
CUT 2

UPPER CUP
CUT 2

FRONT
INFILL
CUT 2

LOWER CUP
CUT 2

LOWER CUP
CUT 2

FRONT
ELASTIC
CUT 2

CENTER
FRONT
CUT 1

BACK ELASTIC
CUT 2

SIDE
FRONT
CUT 2

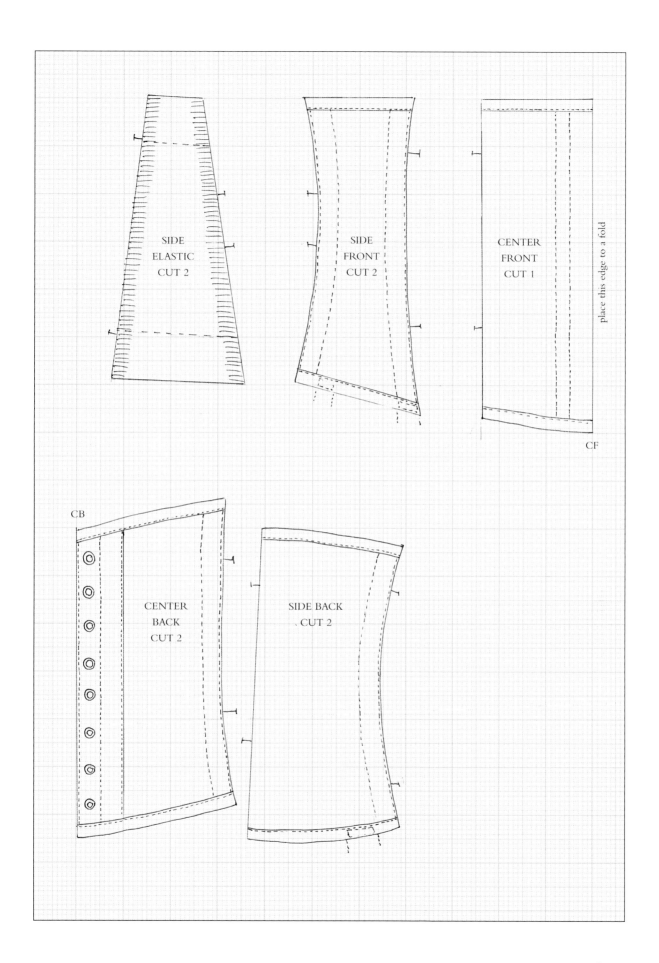

SIDE
ELASTIC
CUT 2

SIDE
FRONT
CUT 2

CENTER
FRONT
CUT 1

place this edge to a fold

CF

CB

CENTER
BACK
CUT 2

SIDE BACK
CUT 2

Beige Silk Slip, 1930–50

This was the most difficult pattern to take and the result will require care in use; cutting on the bias creates elasticity in the fabric that is hard to reproduce in a pattern, and wearing and washing then creates further distortion.

This garment was found in a thrift store and looks unworn. The label states "Regine Brenner 35." It is made from silk crêpe de Chine and satin-backed crêpe with a machine lace trim, which is hand sewn on to the bodice and hand faggotted to the hem. Simple, hand-embroidered flower-leaf-flower stitching decorates the cups. The side seams are machine stitched together then machined on the right side of the garment on the seam, with a silk thread that gives a picot effect. On the inside both raw edges are turned in and oversewn together, while all of the other seams are overcast by hand.

Because of the bias nature of this garment it would stretch to allow someone to put it on, and then it would fall and hug the figure with a fluid grace. This is a very sophisticated shape, reminiscent of the work of fashion designer Madeleine Vionnet, "Queen of the Bias Cut." Whoever developed the original pattern for this petticoat really understood bias cutting.

This garment is made of silk and is non see-through, and the bust shaping is defined. The earliest possible date is 1930 but could be as late as 1950; after this time fitting would have been achieved using fabric with Spandex or Lycra in it.

Left: This silk slip is exquisitely fitted with a bias cut—a difficult task without the use of elasticated fabric.

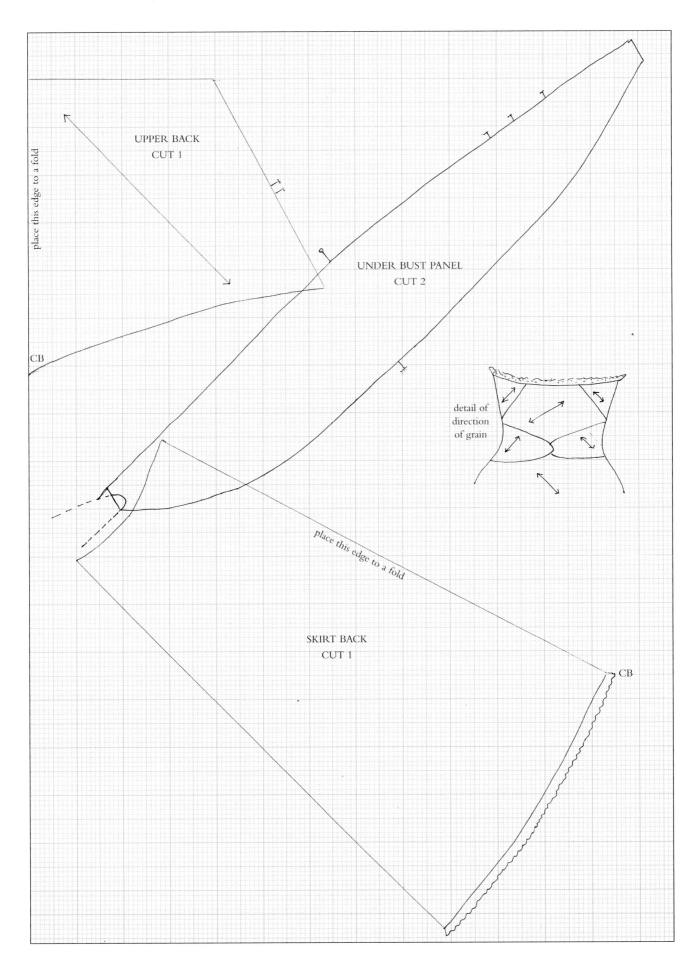

UPPER BACK
CUT 1

place this edge to a fold

CB

UNDER BUST PANEL
CUT 2

detail of
direction
of grain

place this edge to a fold

SKIRT BACK
CUT 1

CB

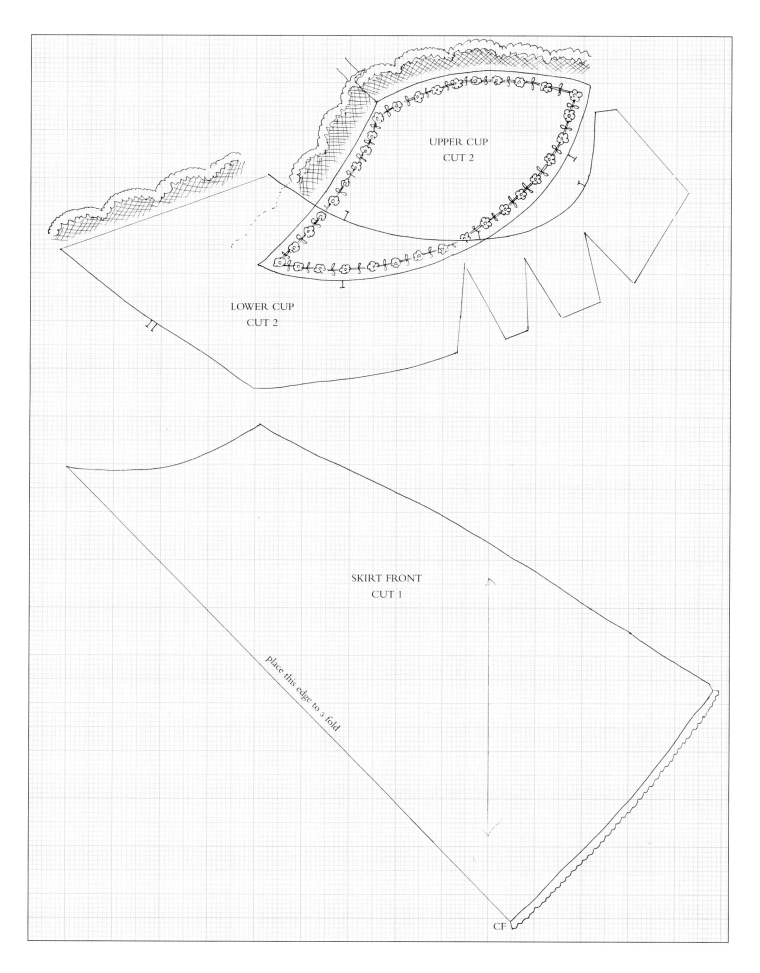

UPPER CUP
CUT 2

LOWER CUP
CUT 2

SKIRT FRONT

CUT 1

place this edge to a fold

CF

Black Corselet, 1950s

This black corselet gives a beautiful shape when worn; the bosom is the regulation "pointy" variety of the 1950s but otherwise it refines the figure and would have been invaluable under the fashionable garments and gowns of the time.

Sophisticated and simple, each panel is made of Spandex with a woven stripe. Spandex, an anagram of "expands", was invented in 1959 by DuPont in America, and its properties of extensibility and retractile force made it invaluable to the underwear, swimwear, and clothing industry in general. Spandex is still used today for its figure-hugging qualities, under different brand names, in many garments for women.

Here the panels cross over at the stomach and the only area that has no stretch is a panel at the center front, which is faced with a non-stretch fabric. Also down the center front is a machined line of silver and black rickrack braid. All seams are turned in and machine faggotted together, creating a very pretty feature when worn. There is no bulk, nor bones, just a little padding for the under-bust, and a low back. This is an elegant, comfortable garment with four suspenders. The wearer would have had to wriggle in and out of it.

The label says "Silhouette made in England 36b" and it has "REJECT" stamped on the label.

Right: A figure-hugging corselet designed to shape and mold the figure into a classic 1950s silhouette.

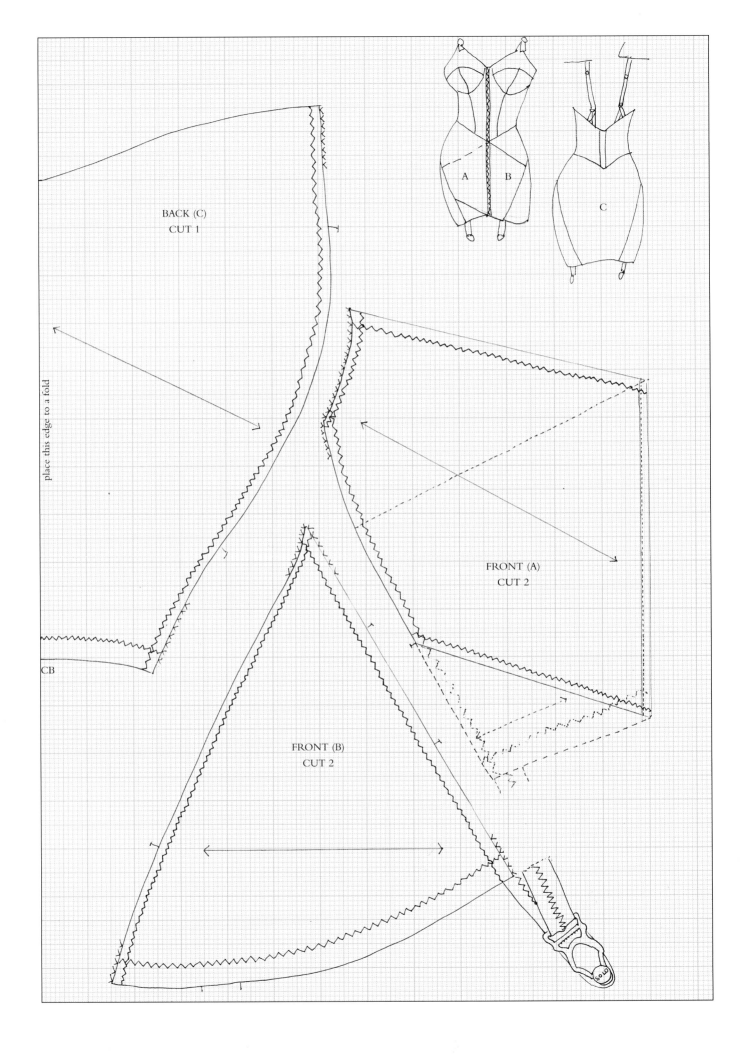

BACK (C)
CUT 1

place this edge to a fold

CB

FRONT (A)
CUT 2

FRONT (B)
CUT 2

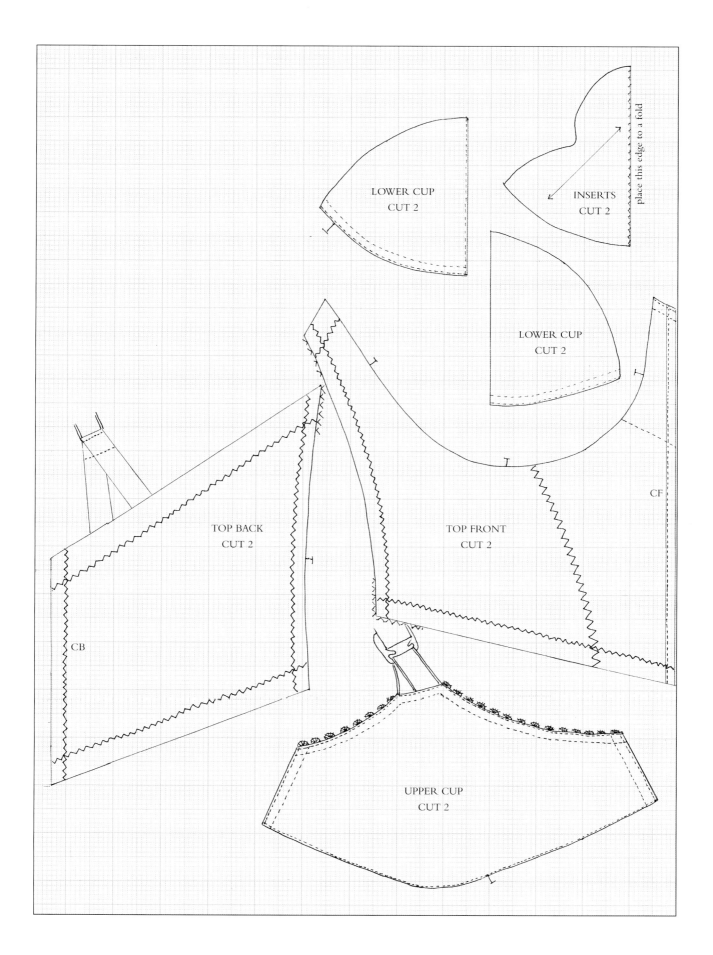

LOWER CUP
CUT 2

INSERTS
CUT 2

place this edge to a fold

LOWER CUP
CUT 2

CF

TOP BACK
CUT 2

TOP FRONT
CUT 2

CB

UPPER CUP
CUT 2

Dior-style Brassiere, 1950s

This large, long-line brassiere is made of white nylon lace mounted on a sheer but strong nylon base; some areas are a peachy pink.

Underneath the lower panel of the cup is a hard yellow layer between the lace and the nylon. It feels like plastic—probably gone harder over the years and discolored—and the bust shaping is unrealistically "pointy." All the edges are finished with a pretty nylon lace; the hook-and-eye tape at the back is faced with a lovely piece of plush to prevent chafing. The decoration on the center front panel is of criss-crossed narrow pink velvet ribbon.

The label proclaims this garment to be:

La gaine CHRISTIAN DIOR
GAINES ET GORGES
PARIS

Another label states "DIOR Model 245/c CUP with Bri Nylon use a cool iron."

Symington's made underwear for Dior from 1957–9. Each garment had a lattice of velvet ribbon down the center front panel; they were available in black, white, and baby pink. Philip Warren in *Foundations of Fashion* (see Further Reading, page 124) said that "all the range featured the recently introduced Velcro to fasten," so this garment might not have been made by Symington's, but by one of their subsidiary companies, which took over the contract in 1959.

This brassiere has no natural fiber in it. After World War II there was a huge change in what fabrics and fibers were used, and these new fabrics had properties that could be utilized and exploited by the lingerie industry.

Far left: A highly decorative Dior-style bra from the 1950s.

Left: This nylon brassiere takes advantage of the new fabrics available after World War II.

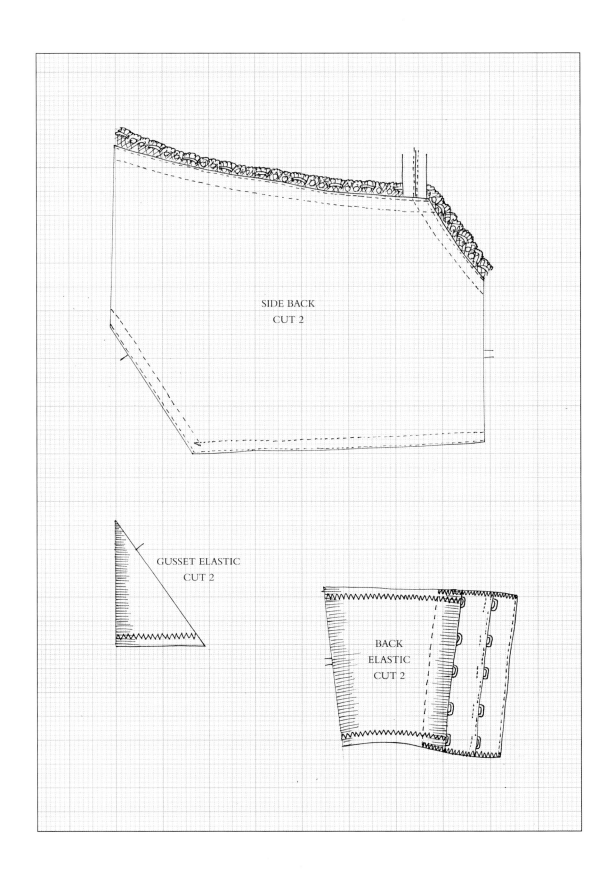

SIDE BACK
CUT 2

GUSSET ELASTIC
CUT 2

BACK
ELASTIC
CUT 2

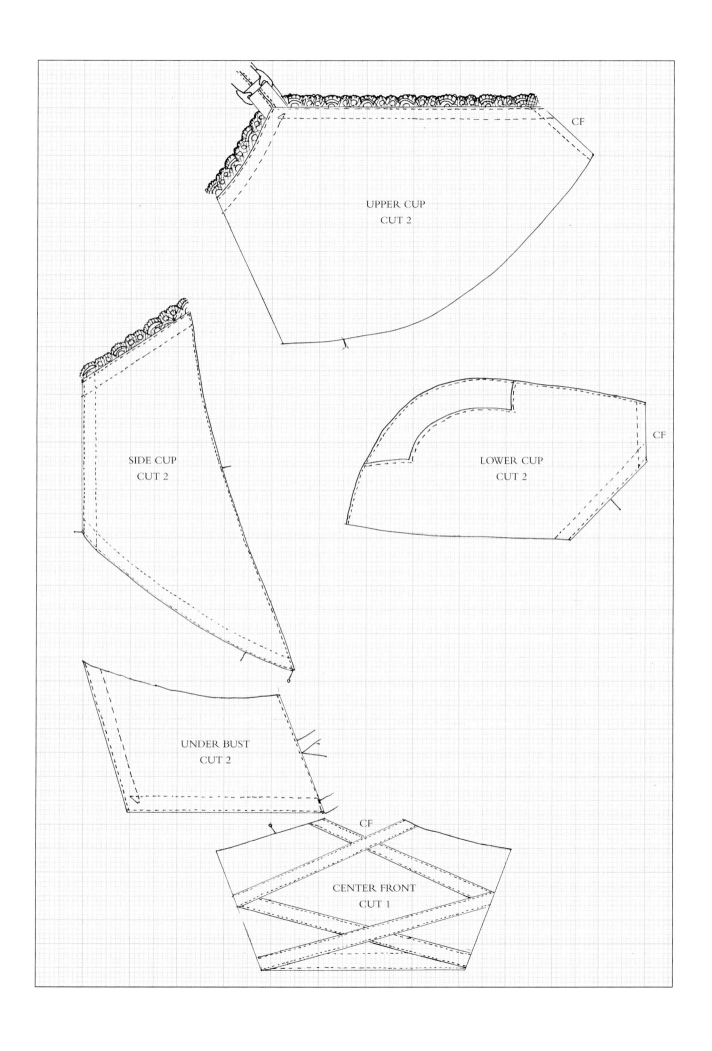

UPPER CUP
CUT 2

CF

SIDE CUP
CUT 2

LOWER CUP
CUT 2

CF

UNDER BUST
CUT 2

CF

CENTER FRONT
CUT 1

Spirella Fitting Corset, 1960s

This corset has been included here as an interesting curiosity. When making a garment, especially a corset, it is best to create a toile, but this is a lengthy business and adds to the cost of whatever is being produced. On the surface of this garment tape is stitched at 1in (2.5cm) intervals. This was to thread the measuring tape through so that the measurements were always taken at the correct place.

Spirella used to employ trained fitters who would visit customers in their homes to "fit" their corsets, noting down the correct hook-and-eye fastenings and measurements, and then send them off as an order to the factory for the corset to be made. Such fitters were still operating in 1985.

The Spirella company was set up by Messrs. Kincaid and Pardee in 1904, and had factories in England, Canada, America, and Sweden; none of their garments were sold in shops but by their well-trained force of saleswomen, or corsetieres, and they provided an excellent service. They would cold-call customers and happily undress in order to demonstrate how good their corsets were. This "modeling" or "fitting corset" was in use in 1962 and when fitted would not be particularly attractive, but the bespoke corset that the client would then receive would fit beautifully and, judging from archive photographs, was really worth the money.

The bones they used were like the spiral wires that are still in use today, but instead of being a spiral wire each bone is more a concertinaed wire. The story is that the wife of the inventor Mr. Beaman demanded he invent something that would not break and hurt her, and this is what he came up with.

Left: This unusual garment was used to measure and fit women for corsets in their own homes during the 1960s.

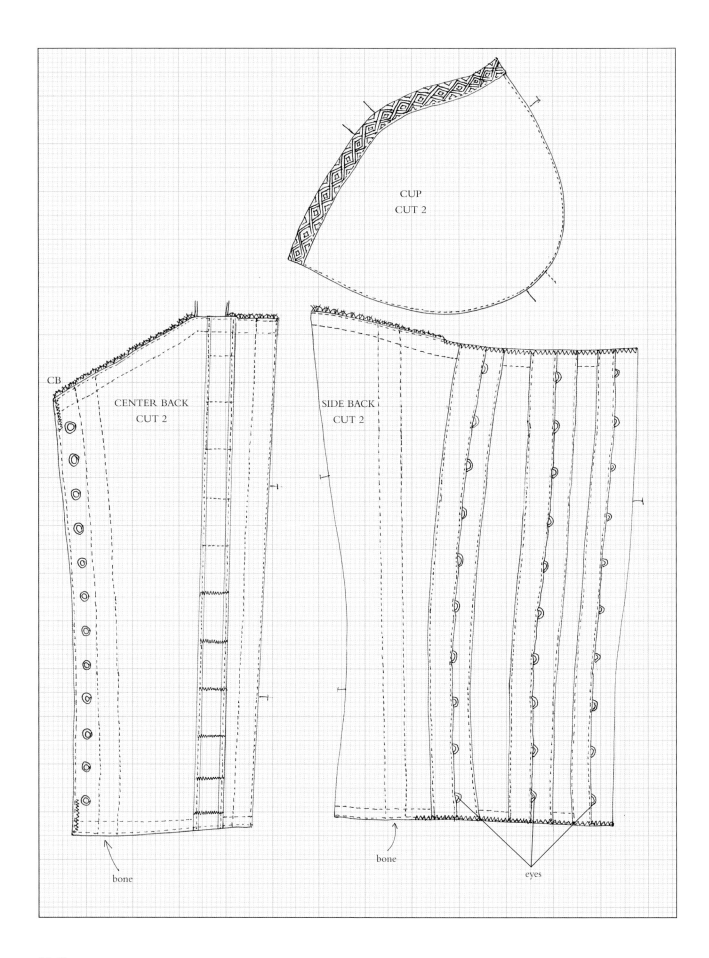

CUP
CUT 2

CB

CENTER BACK
CUT 2

SIDE BACK
CUT 2

bone

bone

eyes

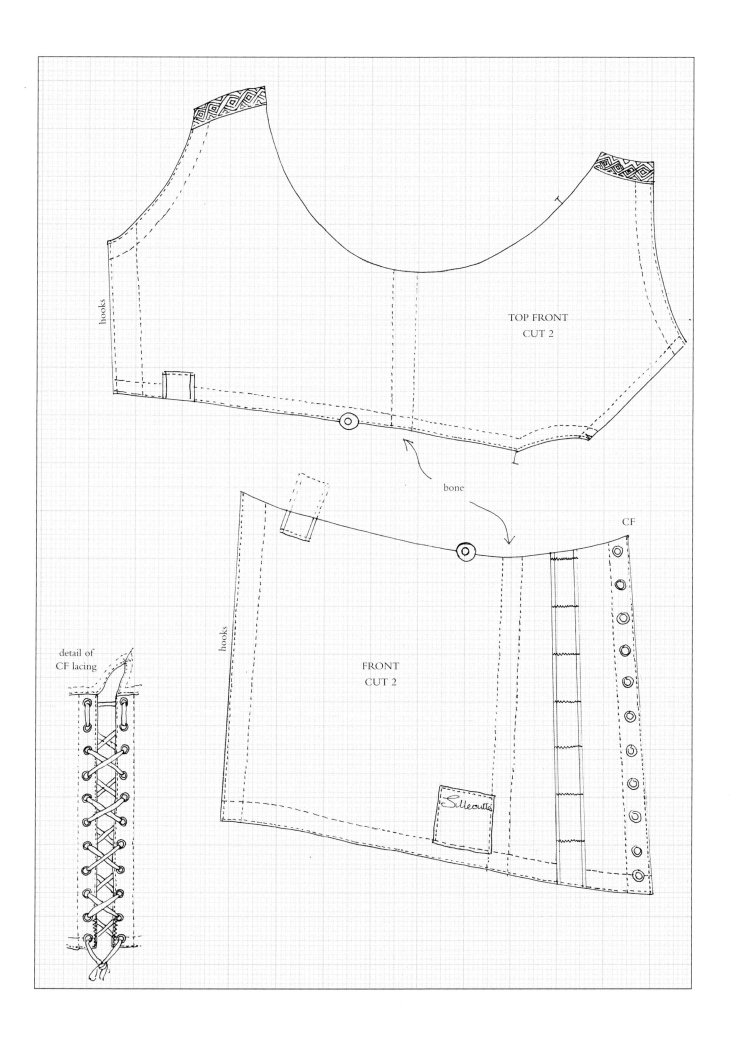

TOP FRONT
CUT 2

hooks

bone

CF

detail of
CF lacing

hooks

FRONT
CUT 2

Silleoutte

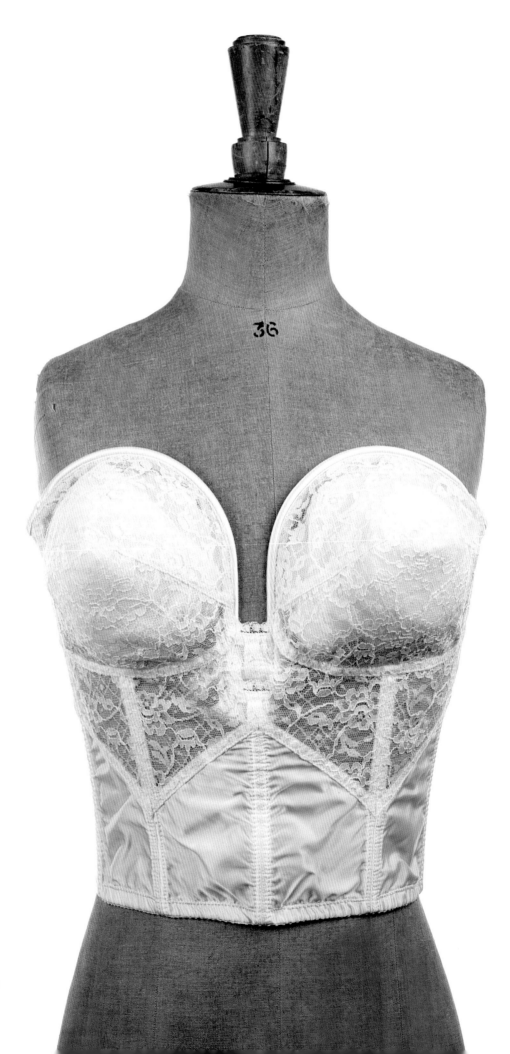

Lady Marlene Long-line Brassiere, 1970s

This strapless long-line brassiere or basque has an overwire rather than an underwire, but will not creep down the body with wear, unlike the 1950s strapless brassiere (see page 74). This 1970s garment is held in place by several types of elastic including Spandex; it is boned and has a beautiful structure. The bone ends are cushioned and the lace is pretty. Such a garment was inspired by what was being seen on cinema screens at the time.

The label says "BY LADY MARLENE, MADE IN THE USA 38C Rigid fabric 100% Nylon Elastic Nylon Lycra and Spandex" and interestingly it has a union label "LADIES GARMENT WORKERS UNION ILGWU."

The ILGWU mentioned on the label refers to the union formed in 1900 to help the workers, mainly female, in the women's garment industry. In 1909 they went on strike for six weeks, resulting in their working week being reduced from 60 to 50 hours; the establishment of a minimum wage; overtime paid and four days paid holidays a year. Employers also agreed to cover all material expenses and power; there was a ban on child labor; wage scale boards would standardize wages; and a label identifying garments as union made was introduced, as on this brassiere.

Left: An example of American vintage lingerie; this garment is from the 1970s.

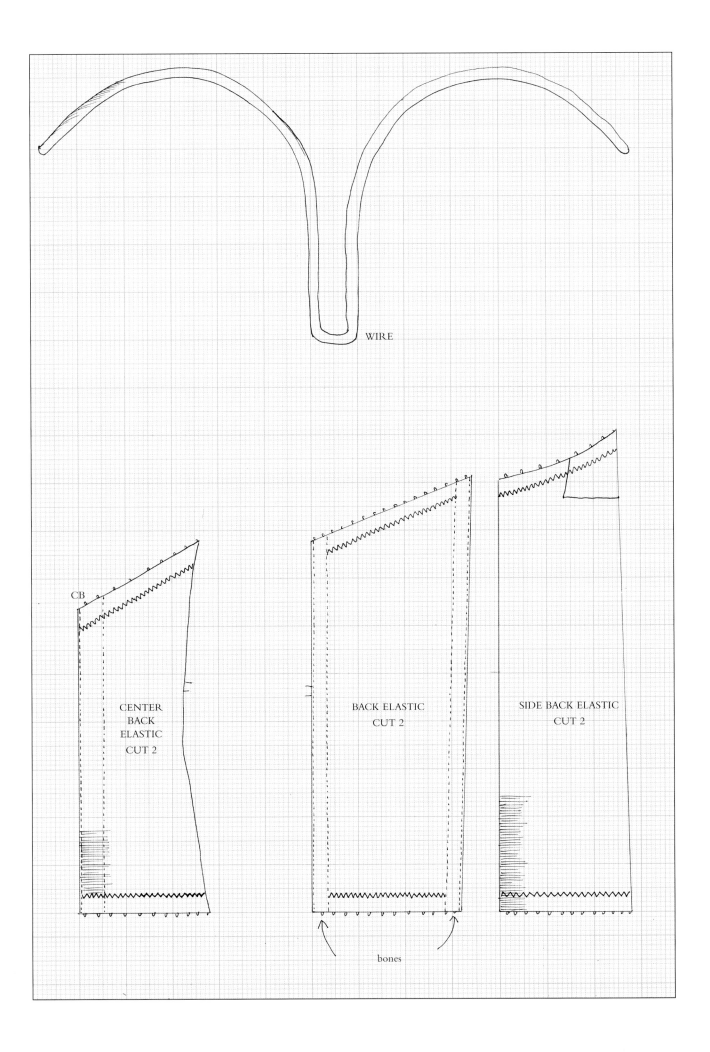

WIRE

CB

CENTER
BACK
ELASTIC
CUT 2

BACK ELASTIC
CUT 2

SIDE BACK ELASTIC
CUT 2

bones

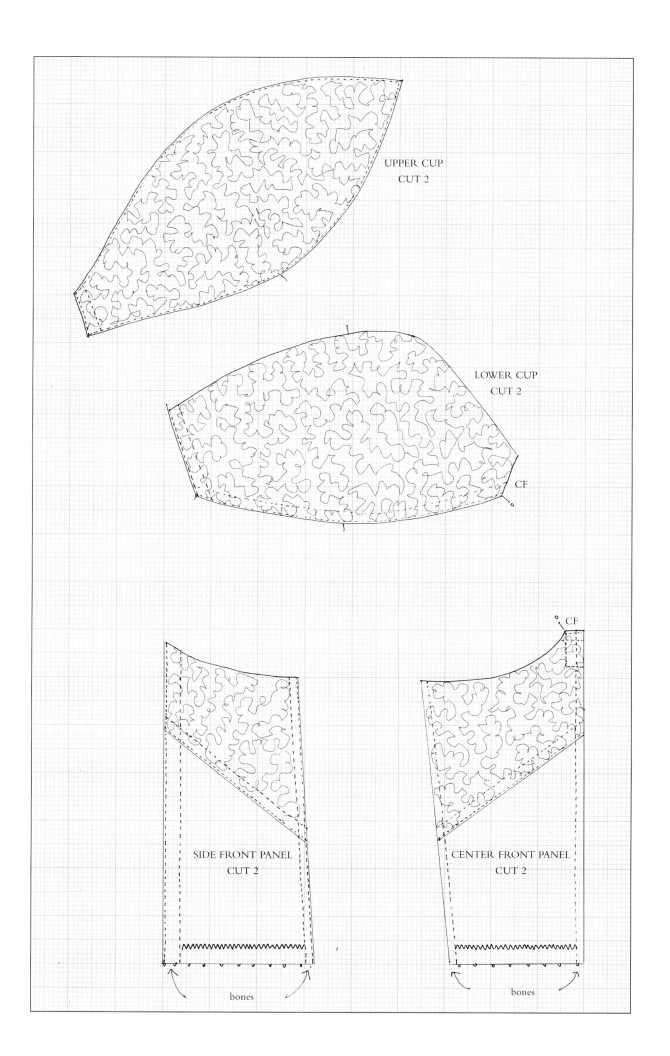

UPPER CUP
CUT 2

LOWER CUP
CUT 2

CF

CF

SIDE FRONT PANEL
CUT 2

CENTER FRONT PANEL
CUT 2

bones

bones

Gossard Long-line Brassiere, 1970s

This Gossard long-line bra is a seductive and lovely garment that today's young woman would have no problem wearing as outerwear.

Today, black lace would send a message—not as it would have been 100 years ago one of mourning, but of availability. Black has changed its meaning so dramatically over the years, after Lana Turner starred in the 1952 film *The Merry Widow* in which she, as the widow, spent a great deal of her time appearing in her very pretty black underwear. From this time black lace underwear became very popular; conveying an impression that the wearer had sexual knowledge. However, it is possible that Madonna in her Jean Paul Gaultier tea-rose colored corset for the 1990 *Blonde Ambition* tour has turned the tables again.

This brassiere has rigid fabric panels, except for the center back panels that close the garment with hook-and-eye tape. There are hoops on the top edge at both front and back, so adjustable straps would have been available for this garment.

Right: This 1970s brassiere from Gossard is made from black lace.

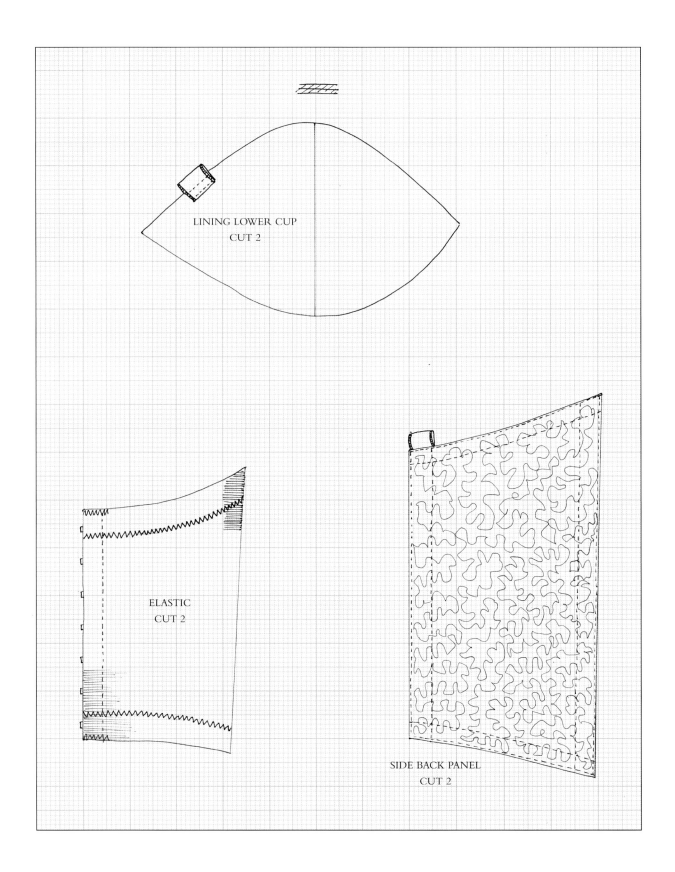

LINING LOWER CUP
CUT 2

ELASTIC
CUT 2

SIDE BACK PANEL
CUT 2

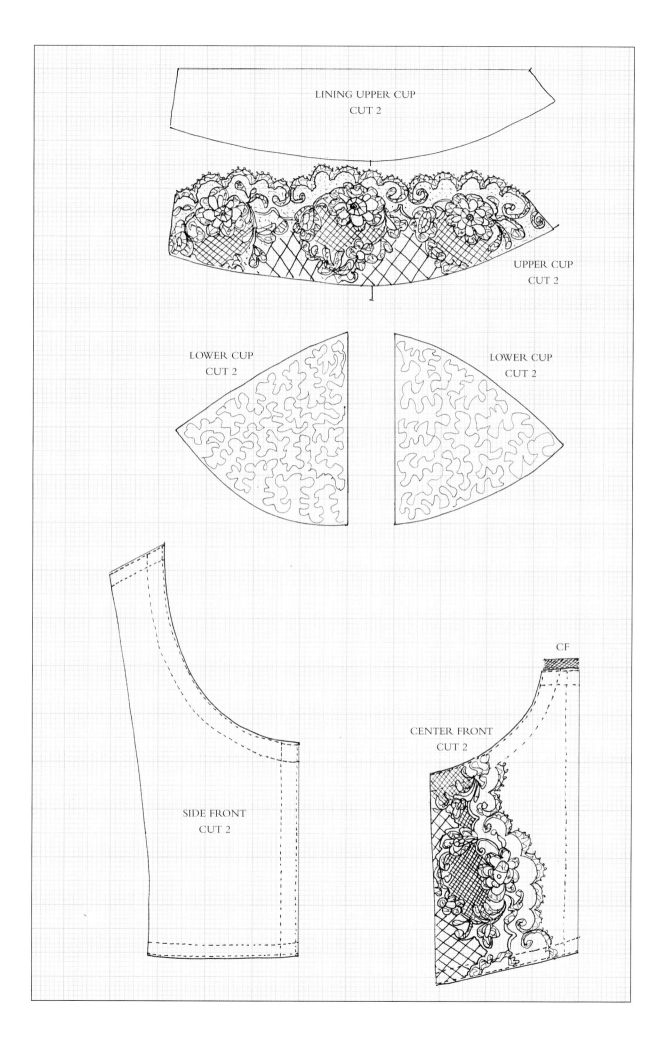

LINING UPPER CUP
CUT 2

UPPER CUP
CUT 2

LOWER CUP
CUT 2

LOWER CUP
CUT 2

CF

CENTER FRONT
CUT 2

SIDE FRONT
CUT 2

Project: Black Brassiere, 1930s

For this project I decided on a simple brassiere that echoes the earliest homemade style, a style that extended through the 20th century. It is similar to a silk and chiffon Kestos brassiere (see page 107), which was made by Symington's and was in production in the 1930s. I have included the pattern for the Kestos bra (see page 104, but no making up instructions in this case) from the St Fagans: National History Museum in Wales.

This bra is made of two layers of a strong cotton tulle or netting, but it could be reproduced in anything lightweight and pliable. The shape is not as sophisticated as we are used to today.

You will need:

Thread
½yd (45cm) tulle, netting or similar
21in (53cm) x ⅜in (9mm) wide grosgrain ribbon
4in (10cm) x ⅜in (9mm) or ½in (1cm) elastic with pre-formed
   buttonholes
2 x 13in (32cm) x ⅜in (9mm) ribbons for cross-back
2 x 17in (42cm) x ⅜in (9mm) wide ribbons for shoulder straps
15½in (39cm) x ⅜in (9mm) wide ribbon for under-bust
24in (60cm) x ⅜in (9mm) wide lace, ⅛in (3mm) of the width
   is grosgrain-like, which stops any stretching of the tulle or netting
Two small, flat buttons

Step by step:

1. Cut out the brassiere shape four times—remember to add seam allowances. (None of the patterns in this book have seam allowances.)

2. Use two layers as one layer, so tack or machine them flat together just inside the seam allowance.

3. Create the dart, press towards the back and then stitch down on the right side to hold the dart folding in that direction, then trim the tulle or netting down to the machined edge.

4. Create the seam at the center front in the same way as the dart.

5. Turn under the top edge of the brassiere, lay the lace trim underneath and stitch on the folded edge of the tulle or netting,

Right: This simple black brassiere from the 1930s can be made from tulle or netting and ribbon.

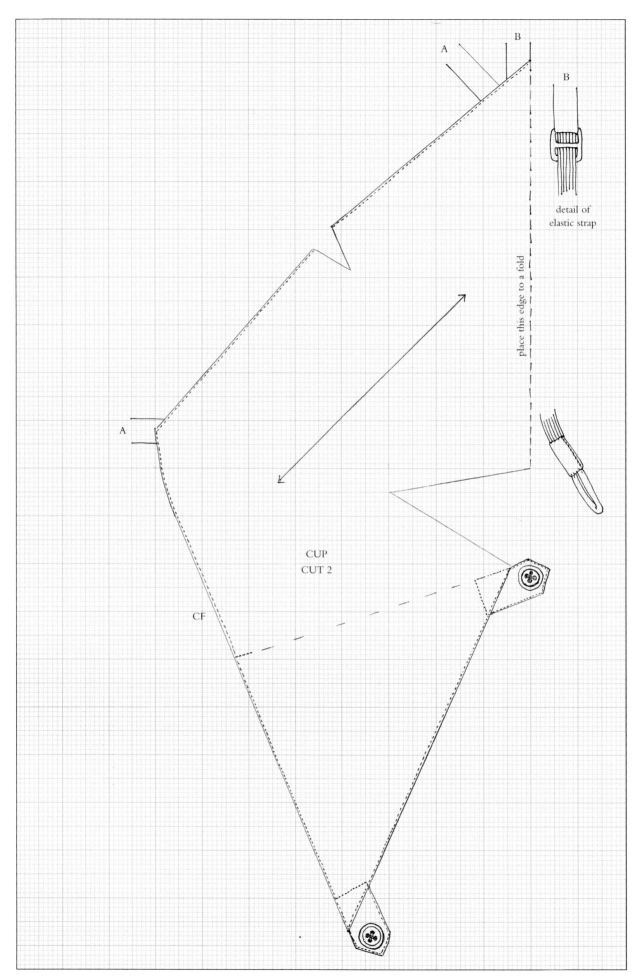

A

B

B

detail of
elastic strap

place this edge to a fold

CUP
CUT 2

CF

A

Kestos brassiere

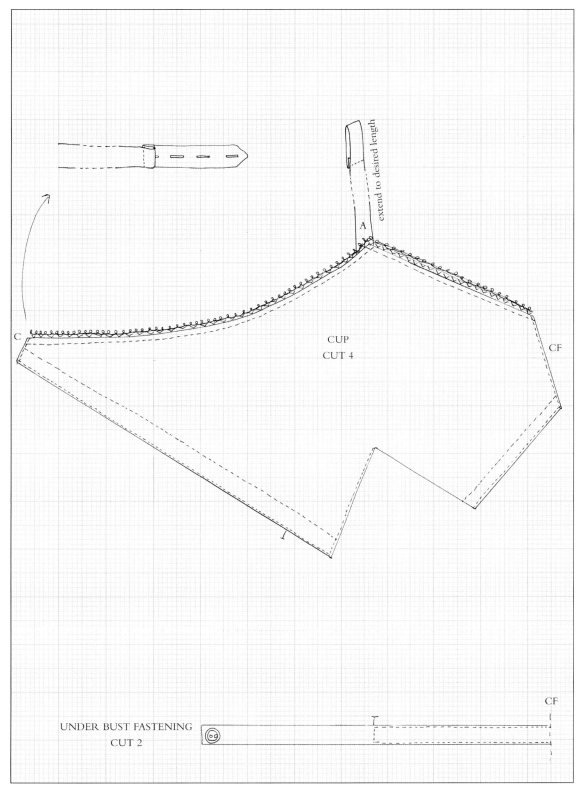

extend to desired length

A

C

CUP
CUT 4

CF

UNDER BUST FASTENING
CUT 2

CF

Black brassiere

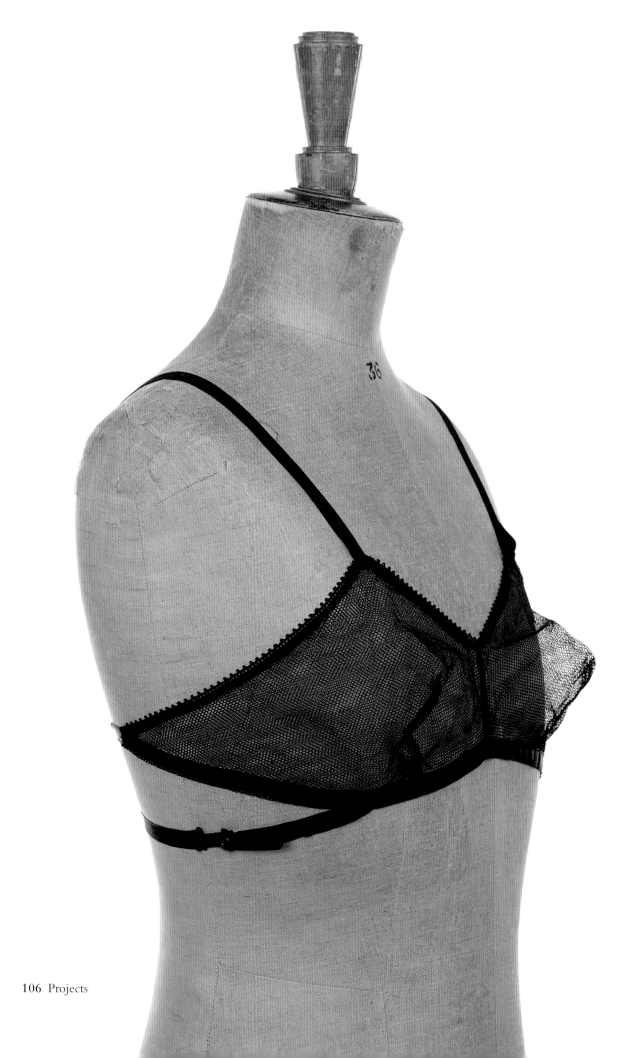

then stitch again ⅛in (3mm) away, trim the excess tulle or netting. The lace disguises the raw edge, and this cotton lace does not fray, so possibly this is why it was chosen.

6. Attach the ribbon shoulder straps to the apex of the bra cup (A). At 15in (42cm) turn the ribbon back, machine at 1in (2.5cm), creating a loop.

7. For the lower edge of the brassiere (under-bust), lay the grosgrain onto the right side of the garment to the seam line and stitch along here, then fold up the grosgrain to the inside of the garment. Press and stitch this down, trim off any spare tulle or netting; the lower edge of the garment is now supported.

8. On the right side of the garment, attach the 14in (35cm) length of ribbon, first having placed the center of the ribbon to the center front of the bra, then machine it, either side of the ribbon, flat to garment, from bust dart to bust dart.

9. Attach buttons to both of the turned in ends of this ribbon.

10. To the underarm edge of the bra (C) attach a 13in (32cm) length of ribbon, to which you have attached a 2in (5cm) length of the buttonholed elastic.

11. Then thread this lower ribbon plus elastic through the shoulder strap loop.

Left: Side view of 1930s black tulle or netting bra, showing the simple button closure feature.

Below: The Kestos bra is similar to in construction to the black net bra shown left (see page 104 for pattern).

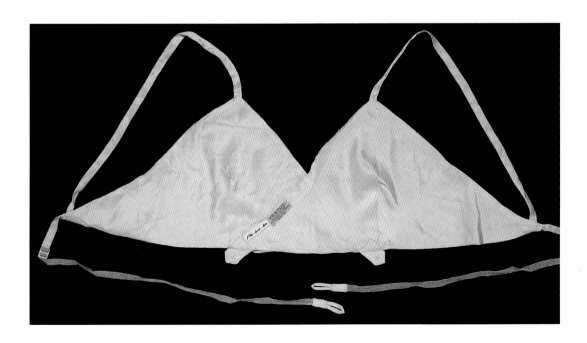

Project: Waist Slip, 1905

For this project I have chosen an example of a simple but delightful garment from the last days of real white waist slips. At the turn of the 20th century white underwear was in decline because of the availability of new fabrics, new fixable dyes and new attitudes. This garment is made of fine, close-woven linen; it has plenty of lace carefully constructed to give the prettiest finish to the hem edge, and flatteringly and economically cut gores to create the skirt of the waist slip, so the garment would always hang with more fabric swishing around the wearer's legs at the back.

You will need:

White thread
Fine cotton or linen closely woven fabric
2 x 30in (76cm) white straight tape or cotton ribbons
70–80in (174–203cm) x 1in (2.5cm) wide satin ribbon
65in (165cm) x ⅜in (1cm) wide eyelet lace
310in (790cm) x 4in (10cm) wide lace

Step-by-step

1. Lay and cut out the pattern. Remember, this pattern, like most of the patterns in the book, is ½:1 scale and that each square equals 2in (5cm). There are no seam allowances on the pattern; these can be marked carefully with tailors' chalk or pencil dots. I would add 1½cm (4cm) for the waist edge and the hem edge, and ⅝in (16mm) on the long body seams.

2. Seam the center front (CF) panel (which you will have remembered to cut on a fold) to the side front (SF) panel. Press away from the CF, trim the top layer, the CF panel, to less than half the finished width, then turn in the selvage of the SF to the stitching line and stitch this down. This is a sort of French seam, one that utilizes a nice selvage and prevents fraying. Alternatively, make a French seam.

3. Then add the back panels to the SF panels, using the same method.

4. The center back (CB) seam is a French seam, so place wrong sides together and machine at ¼in (5mm), trim the seam to ⅛in (3mm) and press first to one side, then press with right sides together, encasing the raw edges completely, now sew a seam at ⅜in (9.5mm) and press. This only needs to be done from the balance mark to the hem.

5. To create the CB opening, turn each raw edge in twice, to the inside of the garment and machine on the fold.

6. To create the waistband; turn in and press at ½in (1cm) along all the waist edge, then turn in again, this time at 1in (2.5cm) and press. This time the CF will narrow to being only ½in (1cm), because the waistline is curved. Then machine the folded edge. As you machine, catch one end of the 30in (76cm) cotton ribbon where the SF and CF seam is, allowing the tape to travel down the channel. This will form the simple drawstring waistband.

7. Create the hem in a similar way to the waistband; press ½in (1cm) and then 1in (2.5cm) and then machine on the fold.

8. Tack a line on the skirt at 12in (30cm) up from the hem to act as a guide for applying the lace ruffle, and eventually the 1½in (4cm) eyelet tape. This line can be moved; work out how deep your lace is going to be, then mark your line.

9. How much do you gather your lace (or any ruffle)? A general rule is x3 the finished measurement, but first this waist slip has a separate ruffle of 4in (10cm) wide lace on the hem. In this case, 110in (275cm) of lace has been very gently gathered, pinned and then sewn 4in (10cm) above the hem edge of 74in (188cm).

10. The top ruffle is three widths of lace joined together, top to bottom, top to bottom, to create a ruffle 12in (30cm) deep. In this case 190in (480cm) of ruffle is gathered to fit onto 60in (152cm) following the x3 rule; after this is pinned and machined, apply the eyelet lace, stitched top and bottom. Finally, thread the 1in (2.5cm) wide ribbon through and tie in a bow.

To wear; draw the cotton ribbons at the waist up tight and tie in a bow. The waist adjusts from 16in (40cm) to 42in (106cm) so this waist slip could have been for life. It is a versatile as well as attractive garment.

Left: A simple but pretty waist slip from the turn of the century.

Right: Close up detail of the layers of lace that decorate the hem.

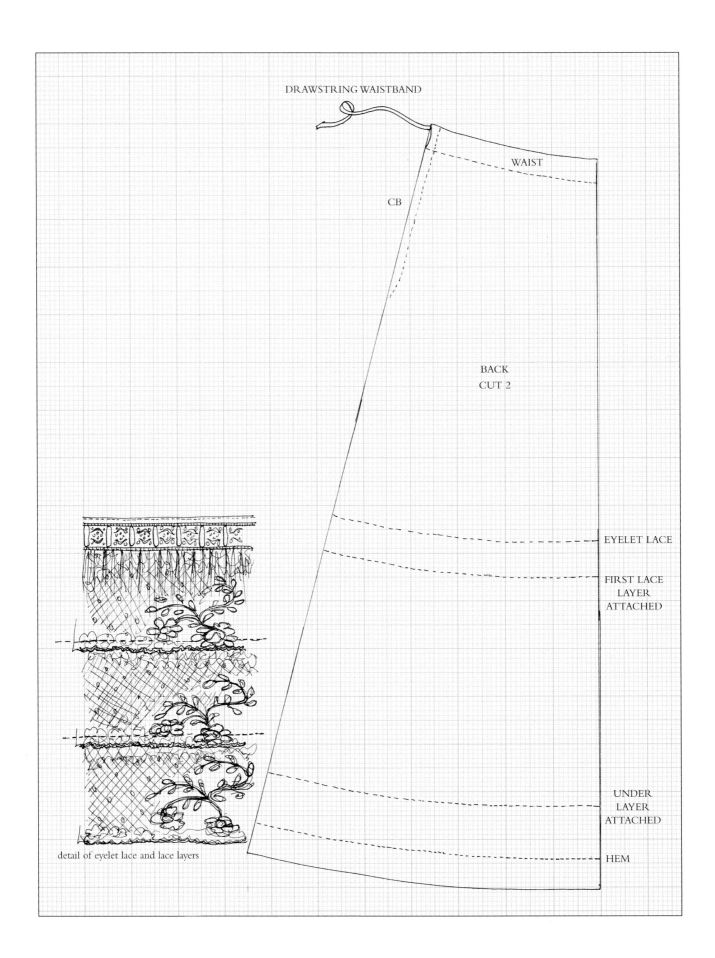

DRAWSTRING WAISTBAND

CB

WAIST

BACK
CUT 2

EYELET LACE

FIRST LACE
LAYER
ATTACHED

UNDER
LAYER
ATTACHED

HEM

detail of eyelet lace and lace layers

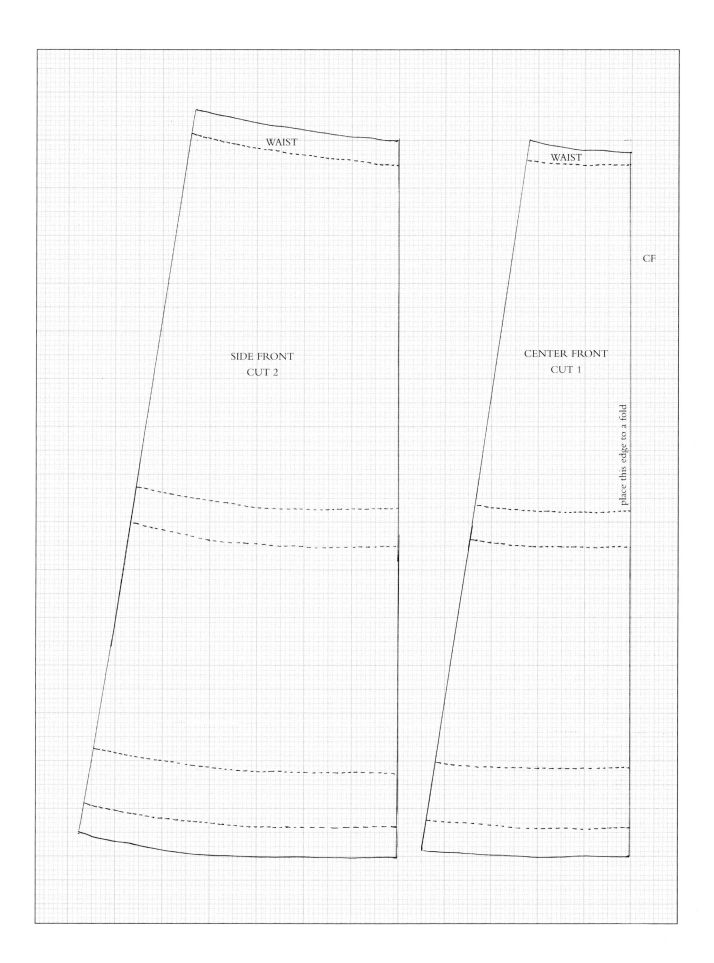

WAIST

WAIST

CF

SIDE FRONT
CUT 2

CENTER FRONT
CUT 1

place this edge to a fold

Techniques

Whenever possible, use natural threads when sewing natural fabric and synthetic threads when sewing synthetic fabric for the best results.

Creating the patterns

The scale of most of the patterns is 1:4in. The patterns on pages 13, 24–25, 32, 48–49, 80–81 and 112–113 are 2:1in. All measurements are in inches (with metric in brackets for information). The patterns can be copied by obtaining 1in squared graph paper and plotting the pieces out, or it may be possible to enlarge them on a photocopier.

The patterns have no seam allowances included, as seam allowances will depend on the maker's requirements, so some thought should be given to this before cutting out.

To learn as much as possible from these patterns:

1   First plot a pattern.

2   Add on the seam allowances.

3   Cut it out of a firm felt or muslin and seam it up using a long machine stitch, matching balance points.

4   Attach some faux lacing and any bones that seem crucial to the shape. Faux lacing consists of 2in (5cm) x 15in (38cm) strips, each comprising a row of eyelets set in tape and supported by boning, which can be machined into a corset or toile for fitting.

Next find someone who fits the garment. Observe how it fits on a contemporary figure and give some consideration to the garments that have to be worn over it. Then consider how the figure of the person who will wear it differs from the person it actually fits.

Very little advice can be given in a book about how to deal with this last step. It is suggested that you look at pictures of the period and decide where it is most appropriate to extend or add in a panel. Here are some points you need to address:

•   Does the waist sit where it should for the period?
•   Is the neckline correct for the period?
•   Is the bust the right shape for the period so, when dressed, a correct silhouette for the period will be achieved?

Balance marks

Balance marks are a guide to where seams should match; they are worth marking on the pattern and then the fabric. When the pattern has been plotted it is also useful to mark the "top" of each pattern and number each pattern sequentially, as it is all too easy to get the panels in the wrong order or even upside down.

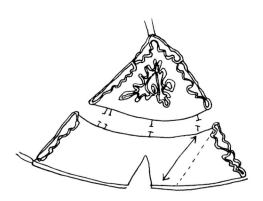

Grain

Most patterns are drawn with the vertical lines of the graph paper echoing the direction of the grain on the corset. Occasionally the patterns do not fit on the page—on those pattern pieces the correct grain is marked with a double pointed arrow (see above).

Hook-and-eye tape

From the 1920s garments we are being closed by this method, which is stronger than hand-sewn individual hooks and eyes, but not as strong as eyelets and lacings. In the 1920s women were not demanding to be compressed into oblivion; a little gentle coaxing, a little securing of the desired outline was all that was needed for the slimmer women, although heavy-duty corsetry was always going to have its place for bigger ladies.

Eventually it would be possible to obtain hook-and-eye tape with three alternative settings for closure. Most hook-and-eye tape is in cotton and can be dyed; it comes in a few different weights, including lightweight and heavy-duty.

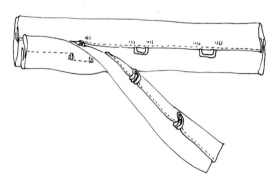

Bias binding

Bias binding was a predominant finish in the 1930s and 40s. You can make your own bias binding with a turner from a commercial manufacturer such as Clover. Cotton bias binding is also commercially available in every color.

Looking at the garments in my collection: on one the edge appears to be turned in to the wrong side, then two rows of machine stitches are executed on both edges of the bias; occasionally bone channels are of bias binding, in which case the boning is extremely light and often encased in cardboard or there is a layer of a stiff voile-like fabric included in the process.

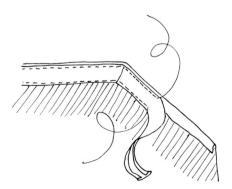

French seam

A French seam can be executed by hand or by machine. It gives a neat, strong, and tidy finish to the inside of the garment, and withstands repeated washing.

Lay the wrong sides of the garment—with ⅝in (16mm) seam—together, stitch ⅜in (9mm) in with a small stitch, trim down to ⅛in (3mm), press and turn, stitch another line at ¼in (5mm).

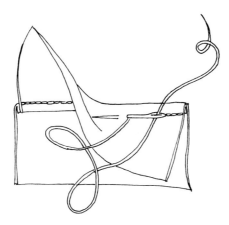

Run and felled seam

The run and felled seam is evident on the 1940s linen knickers (see page 58); seam together at ⅜in (9mm) from the edge then trim down the under-layer to ³⁄₁₆in (4.5mm), wrap the top layer in around the trimmed layer and oversew with tiny hand stitches along the fold. The linen knickers are stitched 28:1in—this intensity of stitching would be damaging to chiffon but is appropriate on linen.

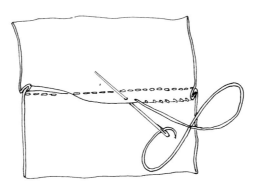

Overcasting

Overcasting is neat over-stitching to prevent fraying and make the garment neat on the inside. It is usually ⅛in (3mm) deep and ⅛in (3mm) apart, and needs a steady, even flow to the stitches.

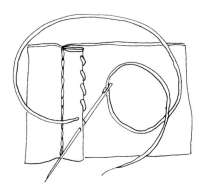

Blanket stitch

Blanket stitch is another means of neatening raw edges by hand, possibly the easiest. For today's garments you would use an over-locker or a zigzag stitch but if it is to be for costume then it is worth doing by hand as it would have been in the past, since the inside of the garment may be seen.

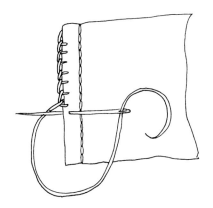

Binding

Binding is not a seam finish for lingerie but an edge finish; depending on the type of fabric it can be as narrow as ¼in (5mm). You are more likely to see this on underwear of the 1920s and 1930s, and handmade underwear of World War II. If it is done by hand, it allows the fabric to fall nicely; if done by machine it becomes a little heavy. Often the quickest route is to machine the binding on and hand stitch it back.

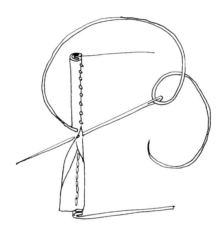

Buttonhole stitch

Buttonhole stitch is easily confused with blanket stitch. The needle is inserted working away from you; create a "knot" at the top by winding the thread once around the needle.

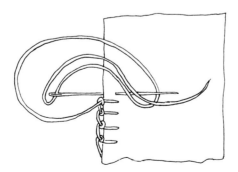

Attaching hooks, eyes or bars

All hooks and bars or loops should be attached with buttonhole stitch; it secures them accurately and is easy to unpick. It should be noted that the open ends of a bar should face the hook, which will prevent the bar bending free in the event of too much stress on it.

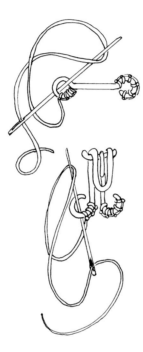

Button loop

The button loop should be executed in buttonhole stitch. It is very useful in lingerie for both buttons and hooks—it will help the fastening to remain concealed and will not chafe or irritate.

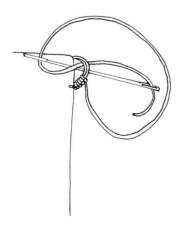

Scallop edging

Scallop edging should also be completed in buttonhole stitch, so that if any of it is damaged it will not unravel. In the past the plain regular curves were often drawn out with the aid of small coins. The edge should be well padded with rows of fine running stitch, which should then be buttonholed over, pressed and then cut. This is the edging used on the corset cover (see page 18) and on the ruffle of the pantaloons (see page 10).

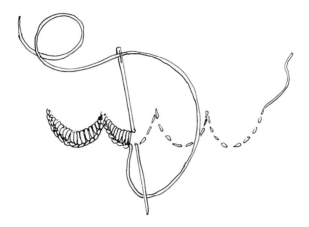

Feather stitch

Feather stitch is decorative and quick to do; it can be found on the leg band of the pantaloons (see page 10). It is blanket stitch used decoratively; you can stitch as many feathers at whatever angle you choose, just making sure that you stitch an equal number of feathers on each side.

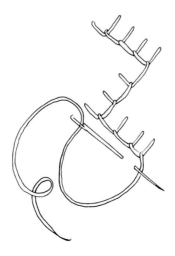

Broderie Anglaise and eyelet work

This is usually worked on white cotton or linen, and consists of a number of worked holes arranged in a pattern. The corset cover (see page 18) offers a good example. The holes are used in conjunction with satin stitch, stem stitch, and overstitch and these connect the eyelet design into a united whole. To create an eyelet hole, pierce with an awl—it does not break the threads but just prises them apart—and then over-sew the edge firmly.

If an oval is desired, stitch around the space with running stitch, snip the center with small sharp scissors, roll the edges under and overstitch the roll securely—large eyelet holes can be achieved by this method.

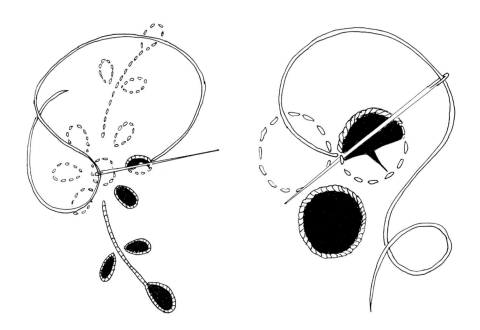

Faggotting

This is a decorative method of joining two pieces of material together; these could be a rouleau loop or a band of lace. It was often used for making entire collars and cuffs by connecting lengths of rouleaus in patterns.

If you have two finished edges that you wish to join, tack the material right-side up' on to strong paper; the tacking should be small and only ⅟₁₆in (1.5mm) away from the edge of the material. The stitching can be as simple as in the diagram, but there are many more fancy stitches you can try.

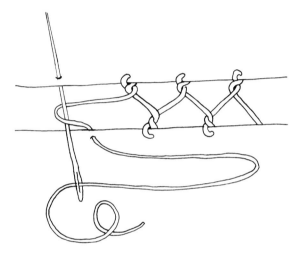

Appliqué and decoupage

Both these processes are worked with contrasting materials; the contrast might be color or, more usually in lingerie, texture, such as tulle or netting and silk on the 1920s bra and knickers (see page 30).

In appliqué the contrasting fabric is stitched on top of another, while in decoupage it is applied underneath and then the top fabric is cut away to reveal it. Very effective embellishments can be made with the outline of the appliqué or decoupage done in satin stitch.

appliqué

decoupage

Further Reading

Altman. B & Co., *1920s Fashions from B. Altman & Co.* (Dover Publications, 1999)

Anon., *The Workwoman's Guide: by A Lady* (Piper Publishing, 2002)

Bell, Q., *On Human Finery* (Hogarth Press, 1947)

Blum, S. (Editor), *Everyday Fashions of the Twenties* (Dover Publications, 1981)

Burnaby, Frederick, *A Ride to Khiva* (The Long Riders' Guild Press, 2001)

Cunnington, C.W, and P., *The History of Underclothes* (Dover Publications Inc, 1992)

Dorner, J., *Fashion in the Twenties and Thirties* (Ian Allen Ltd, 1973)

Etcoff, N., *Survival of the Prettiest* (Little, Brown & Co, 1999)

Fields, J., *An Intimate Affair* (University of California Press, 2007)

Harris, (Ed), *Authentic Victorian Dressmaking Techniques* (Dover Publications, 1999)

May. T., *An Economic and Social History of Britain 1760–1976* (Longman Group, 1991)

Morel, J., *Lingerie Parisienne* (Academy Editions, 1976)

Pedersen, S., *Bra: A Thousand Years of Style, Support and Seduction* (F&W Ltd, 2004)

Salen, Jill, *Corsets: Historical Patterns and Techniques* (Batsford, 2008)

Sparks, L., *The Basics of Corset Building: A Handbook for Beginners* (St. Martin's Press, 2005)

Summers, L., *Bound to Please* (Berg, 2001)

Tobin, S., *Inside Out: A Brief History of Underwear* (The National Trust, 2000)

Tozer, J. & Levitt, S., *The Fabric of Society* (Laura Ashley Ltd, 1983)

Warren, Philip, *Foundations of Fashion: The Symington Corsetry Collection 1860–1990* (Polar Print, 2001)

Wilson, E. & Taylor, L., *Through the Looking Glass* (BBC Books, 1989)

Websites

www.costumesociety.org
www.cosprop.co.uk
www.keritaylorauctions.com
www.Blindlemonvintage.co.uk
marksintime.marksandspencer.com
museums.leics.gov.uk/collections-on-line
www.yourwardrobeunlockd.com
www.farthingales.on.ca
www.lucysfabrics.com
www.sewsassy.com
www.steinlaufandstoller.com

Useful Addresses

Whaleys (Bradford) Ltd
Harris Court
Great Horton
Bradford
West Yorkshire
BD7 4EQ
tel: +44 (0) 1274 576718
email: info@whaleysltd.co.uk
(Linens, poplins and silks)

Vena Cava Design
PO Box 3597
Poole
BH14 9ZL
email: comp@venacavadesign.co.uk
(Corsetry fabrics and a wide variety of everything necessary for constructing lingerie)

James Hare UK
PO Box 72
Monarch House
Queen Street
Leeds
LS11LX
email: sales@james-hare.com
tel: + 44 (0) 1132 431 204
(Silks of every description)

Barnett Lawson
16-17 Little Portland Street
London
W1 8NE
tel: 0207 636 8591
email: info@bltrimmings.com
(Trims and finishes)

MacCulloch and Wallis Ltd
25-6 Dering Street
London
W1S 1AT
tel: 0207 629 0311
www.macculloch-wallis.co.uk
(General sewing supplies)

Wilh. Wissner GmbH and Co.
PO Box 1432
D-73014 Goppingen
Germany
tel: +49(7161)6817-16
email: info@wissner.de
(A wide selections of fastenings, underwires and other notions)

Farthingales
286 Monteith Avenue
Stratford, Ontario
Canada N5A 2P8
e-mail: lsparks@farthingales.on.ca
tel: (519) 275-2374
(Corseting, fabrics, grommets/eyelets, and tailoring supplies)

Sew Sassy Fabrics LLC
504 Andrew Jackson Way NE
Huntsville, AL 35801
tel: (256) 536-4405
(Fabrics and trims)

Lucy's Fashion Fabrics & Trims
PO Box 822
Van Alstyne, TX 75495
www.lucysfabrics.com
(Fabrics, hardware, trims, and notions)

Steinlauf and Soller Inc.
239 West 39th Street
New York, NY 10018
tel: (212) 869-0321
e-mail: steinlauf@rcn.com
(hardware)

Glossary

Basque: a close-fitting bodice.

Bloomers: in 1850 Amelia Bloomer supported women wearing—and herself wore—baggy trouser-type garments, drawn in at the ankle to give more freedom of movement. This style was not accepted, but the name survived and by the turn of the 19th century women had started to wear this style of garment for sporting activities such as cycling. This time the garment was known as knickerbockers.

Brassiere (bra): an undergarment used to shape and support the breasts, from the late 14th-century French for a small jacket worn under a robe. The term seems to have been first used in its new form in *American Vogue* in 1907. Conversely, the French call a bra a *soutien-gorge* (bust support), as first referred to in French magazines in 1904.

Bustier: resembles a basque but is shorter, reaching down only to the ribs or waist. It is a form-fitting garment for women, which is traditionally worn as lingerie. Its primary purpose is to push up the bust by tightening against the upper midriff and forcing the breasts up, while gently shaping the waist.

Camiknickers: also called envelope chemises as the back seam overlapped. A one-piece, loose-fitting garment that combined a camisole and knickers, worn 1900–40.

Camisole: a sleeveless undergarment for women, normally extending to the waist. Historically, the term camisole referred to jackets of various kinds, including over-shirts, worn under a doublet or bodice, women's negligees, and sleeved jackets worn by men. In modern usage a camisole or cami is a loose-fitting sleeveless woman's undergarment, which covers the top part of the body but is shorter than a chemise. A camisole normally extends to the waist but is sometimes cropped to expose the midriff, or extended to cover the entire pelvic region. Camisoles are manufactured from light materials, commonly cotton-based, occasionally satin or silk, or stretch fabrics such as Lycra, nylon or Spandex. A camisole typically has thin "spaghetti straps" and can be worn over a brassiere or without one. Since 1989, some camisoles have come with a built-in underwire bra or other support eliminating the need for a separate bra among those who prefer one. The development of Lycra led to closer fitting vest tops in the early 21st century.

Chemise: a woman's loose, shirt-like undergarment, a loosely fitting dress that hangs straight; a shift. The word "chemise" is French for "shirt" or "vest."

Corselet: a one-piece foundation garment, usually combining both a brassiere and a corset, taken from its original meaning—"armor for the chest area."

Corset cover: worn over a corset, a corset cover could have sleeves; it would give a pretty neckline under a jacket, and was lightweight, usually cotton, often with whitework embroidery.

Coutil: fabric with a strong, firm weave, used extensively in foundation garments. Available from specialist suppliers.

Directoire knickers: worn over the corset; neat fitting and covered the stocking tops.

Drawers: an undergarment, with legs, that covers the lower part of the body.

Merry widow: a short, strapless corset with half cups for the breasts.

Petticoat: during the first two decades of the 20th century, layers of ruffled and flounced petticoats fell out of fashion; narrow, sometimes tight, skirts became more common. Then, in the 1920s, chiffon dresses needing opaque petticoat slips became fashionable. In the 1930s, narrow skirts returned and petticoats again were unpopular until the end of the decade when they were revived for some evening, prom and wedding gowns. World War II rationing again brought an end to petticoats. They were revived by Christian Dior for his full-skirted "New Look" of 1947 and tiered, ruffled, and stiffened petticoats remained extremely popular during the 1950s, especially with teenage girls. Most of these petticoats were tulle- or netting-like crinoline, or sometimes made of horsehair. Increasingly, nylon chiffon, taffeta, and organdy were used.

Slip: a woman's undergarment, usually of dress length with shoulder straps, made from a variety of fabrics. In the UK this garment tends to be referred to as a petticoat; in the USA the term "slip" or "princess slip" is more usual.

Index